THE IMPORTANCE OF

# Harry Houdini

These and other titles are included in The Importance Of
biography series:

| | |
|---|---|
| Alexander the Great | Thomas Jefferson |
| Muhammad Ali | Chief Joseph |
| Louis Armstrong | Malcolm X |
| Napoleon Bonaparte | Margaret Mead |
| Rachel Carson | Michelangelo |
| Cleopatra | Wolfgang Amadeus Mozart |
| Christopher Columbus | Sir Isaac Newton |
| Marie Curie | Richard M. Nixon |
| Thomas Edison | Louis Pasteur |
| Albert Einstein | Jackie Robinson |
| Benjamin Franklin | Anwar Sadat |
| Galileo Galilei | Margaret Sanger |
| Martha Graham | John Steinbeck |
| Stephen Hawking | Jim Thorpe |
| Jim Henson | Mark Twain |
| Harry Houdini | H.G. Wells |

# Harry Houdini

by
Adam Woog

Lucent Books, P.O. Box 289011, San Diego, CA 92198-9011

*Acknowledgments*

Special thanks to Frank W. Dailey and the Society of American Magicians for providing photographs. Membership in the Society of American Magicians' Young Members Program, which includes a monthly newsletter, is open to young people seven through sixteen years of age. For more information contact:

Margaret Dailey, P.N.P.
7101 Buick Drive
Indianapolis, IN 46214-3224

Library of Congress Cataloging-in-Publication Data

Woog, Adam, 1953-
    Harry Houdini / by Adam Woog
        p. cm. — (The Importance of)
    Includes bibliographical references and index.
    ISBN 1-56006-053-0 (acid-free paper)
    1. Houdini, Harry, 1874-1926—Juvenile literature. 2. Magicians—United States—Biography—Juvenile literature. [1. Houdini, Harry, 1874-1926. 2. Magicians.] I.Title. II. Series.
GV1545.H8W66     1995
793.8'092—dc20
[B]                                 93-47622
                                      CIP
                                       AC

# Contents

Foreword     7
Important Dates in the Life of Harry Houdini     8

**INTRODUCTION**
*The Best-Remembered Magician*     9

**CHAPTER 1**
*Houdini's Early Life*     12

**CHAPTER 2**
*The Beginnings of a Career*     19

**CHAPTER 3**
*Europe and Return*     31

**CHAPTER 4**
*From Magician to Escape Artist*     45

**CHAPTER 5**
*Magic and Movies: During and After the War*     60

**CHAPTER 6**
*Exposing Spiritualism*     72

**CHAPTER 7**
*Houdini's Last Days*     86

**EPILOGUE**
*The Mystery Lingers*     94

Notes     103
For Further Reading     105
Additional Works Consulted     106
Index     107
Picture Credits     111
About the Author     112

# Foreword

THE IMPORTANCE OF biography series deals with individuals who have made a unique contribution to history. The editors of the series have deliberately chosen to cast a wide net and include people from all fields of endeavor. Individuals from politics, music, art, literature, philosophy, science, sports, and religion are all represented. In addition, the editors did not restrict the series to individuals whose accomplishments have helped change the course of history. Of necessity, this criterion would have eliminated many whose contribution was great, though limited. Charles Darwin, for example, was responsible for radically altering the scientific view of the natural history of the world. His achievements continue to impact the study of science today. Others, such as Chief Joseph of the Nez Percé, played a pivotal role in the history of their own people. While Joseph's influence does not extend much beyond the Nez Percé, his nonviolent resistance to white expansion and his continuing role in protecting his tribe and his homeland remain an inspiration to all.

These biographies are more than factual chronicles. Each volume attempts to emphasize an individual's contributions both in his or her own time and for posterity. For example, the voyages of Christopher Columbus opened the way to European colonization of the New World. Unquestionably, his encounter with the New World brought monumental changes to both Europe and the Americas in his day. Today, however, the broader impact of Columbus's voyages is being critically scrutinized. *Christopher Columbus,* as well as every biography in The Importance Of series, includes and evaluates the most recent scholarship available on each subject.

Each author includes a wide variety of primary and secondary source quotations to document and substantiate his or her work. All quotes are footnoted to show readers exactly how and where biographers derive their information, as well as to provide stepping stones to further research. These quotations enliven the text by giving readers eyewitness views of the life and times of each individual covered in The Importance Of series.

Finally, each volume is enhanced by photographs, bibliographies, chronologies, and comprehensive indexes. For both the casual reader and the student engaged in research, The Importance Of biographies will be a fascinating adventure into the lives of people who have helped shape humanity's past and present, and who will continue to shape its future.

# Important Dates in the Life of Harry Houdini

**1874** — Ehrich Weisz, later known as Harry Houdini, is born in Pest, Hungary on March 24.

**ca.1876** — Comes to America with his family.

**ca.1888** — Reads Robert-Houdin's autobiography and begins to practice magic tricks.

**ca.1891** — First professional appearances.

**1894** — Marries Beatrice ("Bess") Raymond on July 22; she then joins his act.

**1900** — Sails for Europe in May; the beginning of his success as a performer.

**1904-1905** — Returns to New York, buys a house, and plans his return to U.S. stages.

**1906** — Escapes from jail cell that had held presidential assassin Charles Guiteau, in Washington, D.C., and accomplishes the famous "icy river" escape in Detroit.

**1910** — Becomes the first person to fly an airplane in Australia, March 16.

**1913** — Mother dies on July 16.

**1914-1918** — World War I restricts Houdini to performing in the United States.

**1919** — First motion picture, *The Master Mystery*, opens.

**1920** — Meets Arthur Conan Doyle, creator of Sherlock Holmes and enthusiastic spiritualist.

**1922** — Joins committee on psychic investigations sponsored by *Scientific American* magazine.

**1926** — Injured in Montreal dressing room by visiting student on October 22; dies in Detroit on October 31.

# The Best-Remembered Magician

*From Funk & Wagnalls's* New Standard Dictionary, *1920:*

*HOUDINI, HARRY (1874– ). American mystericist, wizard, and expert in extrication and self-release. HOUDINIZE, v.t.. To release or extricate oneself (from confinement, bonds and the like), as by wriggling out.*

Harry Houdini (1874-1926) was the most famous magician the world has ever known. He stands out even among his illusionist peers—a line that stretches from such legendary magicians as Robert-Houdin and Harry Kellar to modern-day sorcerers like the Amazing Randi and David Copperfield.

He was one of the biggest and most influential figures in the show business of his time, and no one since has been able to fill his shoes. Even almost seventy years after his death, Houdini's name is still instantly recognizable; it is synonymous with mystery, illusion, and suspense.

Doug Henning, one of the best-known contemporary magicians, has said that Houdini was the first magician he ever heard of by name. Noting that TV has created audiences that are immensely larger than those in Houdini's time, he writes:

Each of the network television magic specials I've done was seen by more people than saw Houdini on stage in his entire lifetime; yet today, if one were to ask the man on the street to name a magician, he would be much more likely to name Houdini than Doug Henning.[1]

Houdini was, and still is, famous just for his magic. But Houdini also represents much more. He has become a part of the

*Harry Houdini, the most famous magician the world has ever known.*

world's collective dreams. This is because of one particular gift he possessed: a spectacular genius for escaping from seemingly foolproof restraints.

Houdini could escape from anything and everything. You name it—and his audiences did—and Houdini would get out of it. Ropes, handcuffs, leg irons, sealed sacks, locked trunks, coffins, straitjackets, prison cells, restrictive devices from earlier times such as stocks and pillories, iron boilers that had been riveted shut, packing cases that had been nailed up and thrown into rivers, water-filled glass cases

*Houdini's knack for escaping from seemingly impossible constraints earned him a reputation as an ingenious escape artist.*

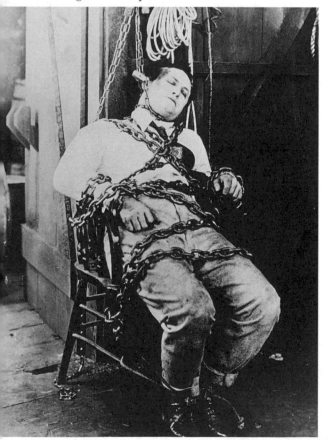

in which he was hung upside down and shackled, . . . nothing could hold him.

His escapes show us that courage and persistence can triumph over impossible odds. He demonstrated clearly that the mind and body can overcome the most difficult obstacles. Even when Houdini's natural strength and agility were augmented with special tools or devices, his cleverness at finding solutions to problems (not to mention his cleverness at pulling the wool over his audiences' eyes) is an inspiration. As biographer-magician Milbourne Christopher notes, "He was, and is, a symbol for man himself—the ingenious creature who overcomes seemingly impossible obstacles by sheer force of willpower."[2]

Who was this man who commanded such power and popular attention? Houdini was a powerfully built natural athlete, but his physical stance alone was not remarkable. He was short, about five feet five inches, with bushy hair, a large head, a broad forehead, and intense gray-blue eyes. His speaking voice was high-pitched, and in his early days on the stage, his language was the tough, ungrammatical speech that reflected his New York upbringing: "Ladies and Gents, as youse can see I ain't got nothing up my sleeve!"[3]

He was short-tempered, quick to take offense, slow to drop a grudge, and almost completely self-centered. He had boundless energy and intense passions, but was almost incapable of taking care of himself on an everyday basis. He demanded complete loyalty from those close to him and was extremely loyal to his friends; but he was also quick to reject the friendship of anyone he thought had let him down.

There are several reasons for Houdini's lasting appeal. One was his tremendous personal charisma. When he walked

## Houdini as Actor

*Literary and dramatic critic Edmund Wilson, quoted in Doug Henning's* Houdini: His Legend and His Magic, *notes that Houdini was interested in "that branch of magic furthest from the theatre."*

"When he performs tricks, it is with the directness and simplicity of an expert giving a demonstration, and he talks to his audience not in the character of a conjuror, but quite straightforwardly and without patter. His professional formulas—such as 'Will wonders never cease!', with which he signifies the end of a trick—have a quaint conventional sound, as if they had been acquired as a concession to the theatre. . . .

He saw himself as a romantic figure. He lived his own drama and had otherwise little of the actor about him—so little that . . . one has the feeling that in his role of public entertainer, he was a little out of his orbit."

into a room, he instantly became the center of attention. His smile was wide and engaging, his gaze direct. When he appeared on stage, he had the full and unwavering attention of his audiences.

He also had a tremendous knack for publicity: he was quick to play up any controversy, and he worked hard to make his performances memorable. The world knows Houdini because he made great copy for newspaper reporters. He also, however, pioneered the use of two then-new branches of the media, radio and film, to make sure his name was always before the public.

Still, the main reason for Houdini's lasting appeal is the power of his escapes. Unlike classic illusions, such as the disappearing rabbit or the woman cut in half,

escapes are real events in the real world. An escape artist is a magician in that we don't know how the miraculous escapes are made. But those escapes are not made in fantasy.

Houdini's exploits were thus events that everyone, from factory workers to royalty, could appreciate. After hearing that Houdini had announced that his "escape secret" was for sale, a convicted burglar is said to have remarked, "I'm afraid we can't come to terms. It would take me too long to steal the money."[4] And when U.S. president Woodrow Wilson came backstage to greet Houdini after a performance, he commented, "I envy your ability to escape from tight places. Sometimes I wish I were able to do the same."[5]

This is the story of the Great Escaper.

# 1 Houdini's Early Life

*Houdini: His Life Story*, a semiofficial biography written by Harold Kellock a few years after the escape artist's death, with the cooperation of his widow, creates an air of glamour and mystery with its very first sentence:

> Houdini began his career with a traveling circus at the age of nine, in the Middle West, and his first trick, which he had perfected laboriously in secret in the family woodshed, was to pick up needles with his eyelids while suspended by the heels head downward.[6]

This was a story Houdini often related to newspaper reporters and others who were curious about his early years. It is typical of the larger-than-life tales Houdini told about himself—and encouraged others to tell. Unfortunately, it is not true.

Throughout his life, and true to the grand traditions of show business, Houdini used such exaggerations in speaking of his life in this way. In this case, the "traveling circus" was actually a backyard affair he put together with a friend, and "the Prince of the Air" (as Houdini called himself then) performed on a trapeze hung from a tree, wearing red stockings his mother had made for him. The eyelids and needles have, however, become permanent parts of the Houdini legend.

## The Old World

Even Houdini's birthplace and birthdate are shrouded in an uncertainty well suited to the world's most famous man of mystery. He insisted throughout his life that he was born Ehrich Weiss in Appleton, Wisconsin, in 1876. Every year, he celebrated his birthday on April 6, because that was when his mother wrote to him with a birthday greeting. His father, he always told reporters, was a lawyer, as well as a distinguished rabbi and teacher of the Jewish religion, who had come to America from Hungary in the early 1870s.

Many of the books about Houdini state these assertions as fact. It was not until years after his death that a scholar of magic tracked down the truth. Commenting on this detective work, Bernard C. Meyer, the author of *Houdini: A Mind in Chains: A Psychoanalytic Portrait* notes:

> Until comparatively recently even the country and date of his birth were a matter of uncertainty, and in some quarters still remain a matter of controversy. . . . It is this very quality of unreliability that is the hallmark of the Houdini story, which from its very beginning is a medley of fact and fancy—

a not surprising state of affairs, come to think of it, in the life story of an illusionist who died on Halloween.[7]

According to the city records of Pest, Hungary, Houdini was born there on March 24, 1874, at the house of his parents at Rakos Arokgasse No. 1. His name at birth was Ehrich Weisz. His father, Mayer Samuel Weisz, was the son of a rabbi from the village of Kesthely in western Hungary. Mayer was indeed a religious scholar and teacher, but there is no indication that he ever was admitted to the bar as a lawyer or ordained as a full-fledged rabbi.

When Mayer was 34, his first wife died giving birth to a son, Armin, who was later known by his Americanized relatives as Herman. According to the family legend, when Herman was a year old, a friend came to Mayer for help in a matter of the heart; the friend wanted to marry a pretty twenty-two-year-old named Cecilia Steiner, but he was too shy to propose. He asked Mayer to act as a go-between, but the plan backfired: instead, Mayer and Cecilia fell in love and married.

The prospects for a poor teacher of religion were few in Hungary, however, and at some point (the records are unclear on the exact date) Mayer sailed for America to seek a better life, leaving his young wife behind. The late 1800s were a time of great emigration from Europe, especially for ethnic groups such as the Jews. Like many others, Mayer was hoping to find work in the New World among people who shared his religion and traditions.

Mayer and Cecilia had several children, but the records are unclear on exactly how many. The infant mortality rate at that time was very high, and only six of the Weisz children survived to adulthood. (Herman also died at an early age.) Ehrich and his older brothers Nathan and William were born in Budapest; Theodore, Leopold, and Gladys, the only daughter, were born in the United States. (The spelling of the family name changed to Weiss after the move to America.)

Houdini later maintained that his father had been forced to leave Hungary, saying that Mayer had killed a nobleman in a duel after the nobleman had insulted

*Mayer Samuel Weisz and Cecilia Steiner, parents of the famous magician, lived in Hungary when Harry Houdini was born on March 24, 1874.*

the Jewish religion. There is no evidence that this really happened. Some biographers have suggested that Mayer was actually Ehrich's stepfather and that Cecilia married Mayer after Ehrich's biological father had been imprisoned for killing a man. Again, however, no conclusive evidence exists to support this story.

Through a friend of the family, Mayer ended up in Appleton, Wisconsin, where he formed a synagogue for the small Jewish population there and was given the post of rabbi at an annual salary of $750. Mayer spoke Hungarian, German, and Yiddish when he came to America. He apparently took a few lessons in English from a Wisconsin woodcutter, but soon gave it up. When Cecilia and the children joined him a short time later, she too declined to learn English. She always spoke German to her children, who grew up using both German and English.

Life for the Weiss family was very difficult even in America. Mayer's views on religion soon came to seem old-fashioned to his new congregation, and after only a few years he was forced to resign and travel to Milwaukee in search of another job.

In his typically melodramatic way, Houdini later wrote of this period:

> Some of the leading factors in the congregation, thinking he had grown too old to hold his position, supplanted him for a younger man, and one morning my father awoke to find himself thrown upon the world, his long locks of hair having silvered in service, with seven children to feed, without a position, and without any visible means of support.[8]

In Milwaukee, the Weisses were always one step ahead of the bill collectors; they had five addresses between the years 1883 and 1887.

All the boys began work as soon as they could, to supplement the family's meager income. Ehrich was no exception. He went to work at the age of eight, selling the *Milwaukee Journal* on the street. He was also a bootblack for a time.

Young Ehrich apparently became interested in performing very early, and somewhere around the age of nine he made his "professional debut"—the trapeze act with the red stockings. His first exposure to a magic show probably came at about the same time, when his father took him to see a traveling performer named Dr. Lynn, "Late of Egyptian Hall, London." Lynn was a plump, gray-mustached magician whose big finale consisted of cutting up a man enclosed in a cabinet, hacking off an arm and a leg and then the head. Lastly, the magician tossed the body pieces inside, drew the curtain—and then, a few moments later, took a bow when the man, whole and unharmed, stepped out of the cabinet.

The Houdini legend became amplified in later years by stories about his early interest not only in magic and performing, but in escapes and lock picking. His mother used to say that he learned at a very young age how to open locked cabinets, so that he could get at the pies and pastries she had baked.

## Leaving Wisconsin

The day after his twelfth birthday, Ehrich ran away from home, apparently restless to see the world. He sent his mother a postcard letting her know that he planned to head for Galveston, Texas, and would be back in a year. It seems that Ehrich knew well that he was too young to head out on his own, because he signed the card, "Your truant son, Ehrich Weiss."[9]

In any event, he never arrived in Texas; he hopped on the wrong railcar and ended up in Kansas City instead. It is not clear exactly where besides Kansas City Ehrich went on his sojourn away from the family, but he did rejoin them in about a year.

While Ehrich was gone, Mayer moved on again, this time to New York City. Thousands of European Jews had settled there in the late nineteenth century, and Mayer hoped that among his coreligionists he would make a better income than he had found in the Midwest. Ehrich joined him, and together they earned enough money to bring the rest of the Weisses from Wisconsin. The reunited family moved into a tiny flat on East 75th Street, about which Houdini later wrote, "We lived there, I mean starved there, several years."[10] The family then moved to another apartment at 305 East 69th Street, which was to be their home for many years.

In New York, as in Wisconsin, Ehrich held a variety of jobs, including department store messenger, assistant necktie cutter, and photographer's assistant. This last job he shared with his brother Theo. It appears that Ehrich and Theo learned their first magic trick, vanishing a coin, from their photographer-boss, who was an amateur magician. Both boys caught the conjuring bug and began reading about and studying magic.

Ehrich was a natural athlete, and he spent his free time (when not practicing magic) running track, diving, and swimming at a boys' club near his home called

---

## Self-Confidence

*In* Houdini: The Untold Story, *Milbourne Christopher comments on Houdini's early reading about magic and early employment.*

"Confidence, he read, is one of a magician's greatest assets. Confidence, he found, was also a great plus in everyday life. Ehrich, at fourteen, was temporarily unemployed. Early one November morning he saw a line of job seekers outside the firm of H. Richters' Sons at 502 Broadway [in lower Manhattan].

Realizing that he would not have a chance if he took his proper place at the end, Ehrich walked briskly to the door, took down the 'Assistant Necktie Cutter Wanted' sign, thanked the applicants for waiting, and told them the position had been filled. The bluff worked. The other boys drifted away. He walked in with the placard in his hand and got the job."

the Pastime Athletic Club. He was talented enough to be awarded several first prizes in junior events. The coach at the Pastime Club advised him to never smoke or drink if he wanted to keep his stamina; this recommendation, coupled with his father's stern religious teachings against alcohol and tobacco, became a lifelong principle with Ehrich.

Ehrich flirted also with acting around this time, speaking his first public words at an amateur theatrical association. He was asked on that occasion to read Longfellow's famous poem, "The Village Blacksmith."

Athletic prowess and dramatic public speaking would prove to serve Ehrich well, because about this time, while exploring his new interest in magic, he found a book that would dramatically change his life. It was a second-hand edition of *The Memoirs of Robert-Houdin, Ambassador, Author, and Conjuror, Written by Himself.* Robert-Houdin was a famous nineteenth-century French magician, originally named Jean Eugène Robert, who had trained as a clockmaker but had gone on to become an internationally known conjuror (magician) and the owner of a lavish theater in Paris.

## Ehrich Weiss Becomes Harry Houdini

Robert-Houdin's book was written in a vivid, exciting style designed to appeal to young men like Ehrich Weiss. It contained many colorful stories that almost certainly had only a little truth to them. Ehrich was entranced, however, and became obsessively interested in the life of the man who claimed them. He would eventually bor-

row Robert-Houdin's name, many of his most famous tricks, and his penchant for embroidering the truth.

A friend of Ehrich's, Jacob "Jack" Hyman, played an important role in nurturing the future performer's interest in magic and the occult. With Jack, Ehrich began making occasional public appearances at local boys' clubs and other places, using props such as cards and silk handkerchiefs because they were cheap. The boys charged a dollar or two per performance.

It was Jack Hyman who suggested that his friend add an "i" to his idol's name, thereby creating the name that would become familiar around the world. Although some biographers have suggested that the name Harry was "borrowed" from Harry

*Ehrich Weiss was obsessed with the life of magician Robert-Houdin (pictured). Weiss eventually borrowed and altered his idol's name to use as his own.*

## Why Houdini Escaped

*Bernard C. Meyer, in* Houdini: A Mind in Chains, *writes from his perspective as a psychoanalyst about Houdini's motivations for becoming what he became.*

"When, in his teens, Houdini gave up his job as a cutter in a necktie factory to become a magician, he revealed an irresistible attraction to the world of mystery and illusion. Yet there were avenues in the world of magic other than the performance of daring escapes that he might have traveled had they exerted sufficient appeal. Nor can his persistence in pursuing that road be ascribed to the prompt attainment of material rewards, for many years would elapse before he achieved success and fame.

Hence it may be suspected that, in choosing to become an 'escapologist,' Houdini was obeying the dictates of his own heart—intuitively he understood the strong emotional component in the public's response to the spectacle of confinement and release. He was surely aware of the widespread human tendency to respond sympathetically to the plight of a man trapped in the accidental cave-in of a mine, or of a child stuck in an underground pipe. He knew that during such crises reports of the fate of the victims dominate the headlines, and that the barely audible voice of a child trapped at the bottom of a well can drown out the combined cries of millions of children dying for want of food. No doubt he could also sense the cruel suffering of those who look on helplessly, and the unspeakable relief and boundless joy that burst forth when rescue is finally at hand. . . .

Whether he was hanging by his feet from the cornice [ledge] of a tall building, risking his flesh while tied to the stake within a ring of burning faggots [sticks], buried six feet below the ground, or plunging from a bridge into the chill waters below, he was not merely playing for publicity, as many people believed; he was living out a dream, an imagined horror that guided the sudden and unforeseen twists and turns of his strange existence, a nightmare as old as human history that linked his tragic fate with legendary figures of antiquity and myth."

*Houdini started his full-time career as a magician at age seventeen, performing up to twenty shows a day.*

Kellar, a famous magician of the era, it is more likely that it is simply an Americanization of Ehrich's nickname, Ehrie.

Thus it was that Ehrich Weiss became Harry Houdini.

## The First Professional Engagements

Mayer Weiss died when Ehrich was sixteen, after making his children repeat a promise they'd made to him many times before—that they would continue to look after their mother, no matter what happened. The following year, Houdini—as he was now called by nearly everyone but his family—quit his job at the necktie factory and became a full-time entertainer.

His first professional appearances included a tryout at Huber's Museum (actually a variety music hall) and at Coney Island, the famous New York amusement park. He was no longer partnered with Jack Hyman, but instead appeared with a strongman named Emil Jarrow, whose specialty was writing his name on the wall while holding—in the same hand, straight out from his arm—a sixty-pound dumbbell. Houdini and Jarrow made their wages by passing the hat to the crowd that had stopped to watch them—a practice known as "getting throw money."

From these humble performances, Houdini graduated to making small tours around the Midwest, performing at "dime museums," amusement halls that offered variety shows at ten cents a ticket. The bills on these shows typically featured such acts as sword swallowers, fire-eaters, comedians, and song-and-dance performers. Typical pay for a beginner like Harry was $12 a week—for as many as twenty shows a day, six days a week!

Harry also began working with his brother Theo, whose nickname was Dash, on a new act: escapes from rope ties. The pair made several appearances as "the Houdini Brothers," including one at the Columbian Exposition at the Chicago World's Fair, in 1893. It was here, apparently, that Houdini learned a trick that would become a regular part of his show: a fellow magician taught him how to "swallow" a handful of needles and some thread, then bring it all out of his mouth with each needle neatly threaded.

But the brothers were still struggling to make a reputation for themselves in the difficult field of show business. It would be some years yet before the world began to recognize the name Houdini.

# 2 The Beginnings of a Career

*Houdini worked hard to establish himself as an entertainer, performing his magic whenever he had the opportunity.*

Ehrich and Theo, the Houdini Brothers (or the Brothers Houdini, as they were sometimes known), worked hard to establish a reputation for themselves as entertainers. They had their work cut out for them; they were beginners in a world chock-full of amusements, and of performers both successful and struggling.

At the end of the nineteenth century, magic was just one of a variety of stage acts that ran the gamut from cheap "dime museums" to lavish vaudeville performances. As writer-magician Milbourne Christopher has noted:

> The first proprietors of American museums had relied on exhibitions of natural wonders and works of art to attract the public. Later showmen, among them P.T. Barnum, added live attractions, freaks, and entertainers, to lure the curious. By [the late 1800s] magicians, sword swallowers, fire-eaters, and contortionists were as much a part of the scene as midgets, giants, and Siamese twins.[11]

The Houdini Brothers performed at any kind of engagement they could find: neighborhood socials, lodge meetings, beer halls. Their mother made them elegant silk costumes, and they even developed a specialty: a trick they called

## On the Road

*The odd circumstances of a beginning vaudeville performer are related in this passage from* Houdini: The Untold Story, *by Milbourne Christopher.*

"Dinner with his fellow attractions was always interesting. Unthan, 'The Legless Wonder,' handled knife and fork with ease, though balanced precariously by Houdini's side. Big Alice, the fat lady, thoughtfully moved to one end of the table so that Emma Shaller, 'The Ossified Girl,' had space to sit as comfortably as an ossified young lady can sit. At Old Moore's Museum, Colonel Goshen, the giant, had Harry on edge. Goshen towered so high that the escapologist half expected to see his face looking down in the cabinet as Theo made the quick switch with him in the box trick. 'In those days,' Houdini said, 'I did not have enough sense to put a cover on my cabinet.'"

"Metamorphosis." It was a variation on the substitution trick—exchanging one person or thing for another in the blink of an eye—which had been performed for many years in many forms by a variety of magicians. In this version, Houdini tied his brother up and placed him in a trunk, which was then locked.

A screen was placed between the audience and the trunk, and Houdini would explain to the audience that he and his brother would change places instantaneously. He would intone, "When I clap my hands three times—behold a miracle!" He would then step behind the curtain, and—presto!—out would step Theo. Theo would unlock the trunk, and—voila!—there would be Houdini. The two boys had indeed changed places in a matter of seconds.

One night, however, a mix-up occurred during a performance at New York's Imperial Music Hall. Houdini made his usual prediction about the miracle and disappeared behind the curtain—but nothing more happened. As the audience became increasingly restless, the stage curtains were drawn and the band struck up the next act's number. It seems that Theo had forgotten to bring along the device that let him open the trunk and get out quickly. After that, Harry was always the one who entered and escaped from the trunk.

## When Harry Met Bess

In any event, the Houdini act was about to change dramatically. Soon, Theo would no longer be a part of it at all. Houdini was about to meet the person who would become his wife and lifelong partner in "escapology."

Beatrice Raymond, who was born Wilhelmina Rahner but changed her name

*Beatrice Raymond was an aspiring singer and dancer when she met Houdini. After they married, she joined his act.*

dentally dropped some equipment when the streetcar lurched, and she helped him pick it up. As it turned out, she was on her way to the same birthday party, and the spilling incident occurred during this private performance.

A third version, however, comes from Theo, who said that he actually met Bess before his brother did. At the time, Bess was half of a song-and-dance act called the Floral Sisters. Both the Floral Sisters and the Houdini Brothers happened to be performing at Coney Island. According to Theo, he dated Bess first and then introduced her to Harry. The mutual attraction was immediate.

No matter which story is correct, it was a whirlwind romance between the two

*Houdini often relied on Bess to help him keep on top of his busy schedules and tours.*

for the stage, was an aspiring singer and dancer—a struggling performer like the Houdinis. Bess Raymond was still a teenager, a tiny young woman weighing less than a hundred pounds, when she met Harry Houdini. Several different versions exist about how the meeting came about.

Bess always said that they met when she was in the front row of a solo show Houdini gave at a school in Brooklyn. According to her version, he accidentally knocked a glass of water-into-wine liquid from his table and splashed her dress. Bess's mother, who was also in the audience, was furious, and Houdini immediately offered to replace the dress.

According to Houdini, he first saw Bess on a streetcar while he was on his way to perform at a birthday party. He acci-

young people. It didn't seem to matter that Houdini was Jewish and Bess was Catholic. The couple were married on July 22, 1894, in a civil ceremony followed by separate ceremonies with a priest and a rabbi. Bess would later remark, "I'm the most married person I know—three times, and to the same man."[12]

She immediately joined the act, and Theo started a solo career, changing his professional name to Hardeen. Bess would tell friends later jokingly that the only reason she joined the act was to keep Houdini from looking at other women. In fact, she was a genuine boon to his act; her small size made her ideal for the trunk substitution trick, and she was experienced on the stage already.

Bess's father, like Houdini's, had died some years earlier. Her mother, a staunch German Catholic, was bitterly opposed to the interfaith marriage, and for several years mother and daughter did not speak.

But Cecilia, Houdini's mother, was apparently pleased with the match, and she got on well with Bess. After the wedding, the couple lived with Cecilia when they were not on the road, a practice they continued until the older woman's death. Houdini would later say of his bride, "She brought me luck and it has been with me ever since. I never had any before I married her."[13]

## With the Circus

In the spring of 1895, the Houdinis went on a six-month tour with a Pennsylvania-

### Bess's Weight Problem

*In Harold Kellock's book* Houdini: His Life Story, *Bess Houdini reminisces about her first appearances with Houdini.*

"In those early job-seeking days I was sometimes more of a handicap than an asset. I was a frail little thing, weighing less than a hundred pounds. The boyish figure had not yet come into its own. It was the period when hips were hips and women prided themselves on bust measurements which today would send them frantically on a diet of carrots and prunes. Even on the meanest stage, the call was all for generously curved Amazons, 175 pounds on the hoof, and the managers looked askance at my uncompromising flatness. Once, when work was scarce in both dime museums and halls, and we tried almost despairingly to break into a burlesque show, the manager took one disgusted glance at me and cried: 'What the hell d'you think I'm running? A kindergarten?'"

based troupe, the Welsh Brothers Circus. Houdini's act at the time included such traditional magic as manipulating playing cards, producing eggs from an empty bag, and changing the colors of silk handkerchiefs by pushing them in one end of a tube and out the other. Bess sang and danced in the act. She also took part in the trunk substitution, which was their grand finale, and together with her husband performed a "second-sight" mind-reading act.

## The Beginnings of a Professional Act

Houdini wasn't content for very long with performing overly familiar magic tricks. During this period, he began to incorporate into his act elements that would mark him as a highly individual performer.

Houdini practiced new tricks incessantly. He needed only about five hours of sleep each night and had a habit of bounding out of bed first thing in the morning, full of energy and anxious to begin work on new ideas.

He kept a notebook beside his bed because he often awoke in the middle of the night with an idea for a new stunt or a new method of doing an old one. He also worked constantly on improving his speaking voice and delivery; he was self-conscious about his rough and unrefined speech.

He was extremely focused on his work and paid little attention to the mundane details of daily life. Bess confessed later that she used to have to steal his underwear at night, just to make sure he had a clean pair; otherwise it would not occur to

him to change his clothes. Often, she said, he would go all day without bothering to eat. When he suddenly realized that he was hungry, he would make a meal out of two quarts of milk with a dozen eggs stirred in.

It was also at this time that Houdini began to work into his act the stunt that would make him famous: handcuff escapes. A well-known magician named Samri Baldwin ("the White Mahatma"), had performed what may have been the first handcuff escape as early as 1871, and several other magicians had included it at various times in their acts.

Nobody, however, had ever done a handcuff escape as the featured part of a show. Expanding his handcuff escape act from a throwaway stunt into a major event would be Houdini's stepping-stone to worldwide fame and fortune. He made a thorough study of standard handcuffs and eventually knew each model inside-out. Some required only a sharp rap on a certain spot to open them. Others could be picked with a pin-size piece of metal.

Houdini spent many of his off-hours in the shops of locksmiths, learning their trade and secrets. He was so confident that he began to offer a hundred-dollar reward to anyone who could handcuff him so thoroughly that he couldn't escape. He never had to pay.

## Publicizing Escapes

Houdini also began planting stories in newspapers of his escapes from regulation police cuffs—that is, standard handcuffs that had not been customized or altered in any way. He would walk into the police

*Calling himself the Handcuff King, Houdini thrilled audiences with his daring handcuff escapes.*

station of whatever town he happened to be in and confidently announce:

> I'm Harry Houdini, the Handcuff King. I'm playing over at the Bijou Theater [or wherever]. I thought mebbe you'd like to see a coupla tricks with handcuffs. Go ahead. Put any pair of cuffs you got on me. I'll show you how I can get out of 'em.[14]

He always got out in record time, and it always made good copy for the next day's headlines—which then translated into better box-office receipts. Once the chief of police in Chicago foiled him by pouring birdshot into the lock of his personal handcuffs, which rendered them inoperable; Houdini was furious when he discovered the trick and afterward refused to put on any cuffs until he was satisfied that they were a regulation set in proper working order.

## The First Straitjacket Escape

A tour of Canada that the Houdinis began in 1896 provided the seeds of several new ideas. In Halifax, Nova Scotia, Houdini staged his first open-air stunt. This is another example, like the escape-from-police-cuffs routines, of his flair for using daring exploits to attract free publicity. On this occasion, he advertised that he would be tied to the back of a "wild horse," bound by a number of handcuffs and shackles, from which he would then escape.

As it turned out, the horse was wilder than expected. Spooked by the escape artist's contortions on its back, the horse took off running. Miles from home, it

*Houdini grins as he is strapped into a straitjacket (left). Using agility and strength, he begins his escape (right). Unlike other escape artists, Houdini performed in full view of his audience, heightening the drama of his performances.*

finally stopped from exhaustion and Houdini was able to release himself. Unfortunately, there was no one around to see him make his escape, and any publicity value the stunt might have had was lost.

Also on this Canadian tour, Houdini visited a New Brunswick insane asylum. Here, he saw a straitjacket for the first time. He was immediately struck by the possibilities inherent in escaping from such a device. The doctor who had been Houdini's guide at the mental institution donated an old straitjacket, and the performer spent days in his hotel room perfecting the art of escaping from it. He found that the extra-long arms, fastened in back, could be looped over the head and undone relatively easily. Great agility and strength, though, were required to undo the buckles, which had to be pried open by sheer strength from inside the canvas sleeves.

When Houdini tried out the trick on stage, however, the audience was unimpressed. The custom at the time was for escape artists to perform their deeds hidden behind a cloth screen as the audience waited impatiently. It was not until some years later that Houdini pioneered the art of making escapes in full view, to maximize the drama. The straitjacket escape was technically very difficult, but—because the performer was hidden—it wasn't exciting to audiences.

The trip to Canada was also Houdini's first exposure to a problem that would plague him as long as he lived: violent seasickness. Houdini lived before commercial air travel, when ocean-going steamers were the norm. For the rest of his life, even the sight of a steamer would be enough to make Houdini ill. He usually spent all his time on board a ship in his cabin, miserable and unable to leave his

*Throughout his career, Houdini endured violent episodes of seasickness on journeys to overseas performances.*

bed. Bess claimed that she sometimes had to tie him to his bed to keep him from carrying out his threat of jumping overboard and ending his misery.

## A Fake Spirit Act

After their return from Canada, Harry and Bess made a tour with the California Concert Company, a traveling show that was advertised on street corners by a "doctor" who also sold patent medicine. Spurred on by the incentive of seeing their name at the top of the bill, the Houdinis were persuaded to put together a "spirit show" of fake mind reading and other psychic phenomena.

Harry prepared for this job by visiting cemeteries in each town, copying down names and dates from tombstones. In restaurants and coffee shops, he listened to gossip about current crimes and scandals. He scoured old newspaper files for stories about past local events.

The troupe also, on occasion, had Bess work as a coat-check girl, and she took such opportunities to look for receipts, letters, or other telltale items in the coats she handled. Information from these sources was later used to great effect when Bess "spotted" (secretly pointed out) the appropriate member of the audience during Houdini's spirit act.

At show time, a committee of audience members would tie Houdini to a chair and put him in a cloth-covered frame cabinet. Thus confined, he would "magically" make bells ring, tambourines rattle, trumpets fly through the air, tables lift up on their own, and so on. Next, Houdini would mysteriously free himself of his ropes and pretend to be possessed by the spirit world. He would give a rousing speech about how he sensed strange presences, with messages coming through that named names and dates and exposed family secrets.

He then would start spouting some of the secrets he had picked up on his rounds of the graveyards, restaurants, and newspaper libraries. He quickly discovered that an audience that had come to see a medium was easily fooled and satisfied with such a show, compared with one that had come to see a magician performing "straight" magic.

Much of the success of this act depended on Houdini's skill and his phenomenal memory, but sometimes sheer luck played a part as well. Once he recognized in the audience a woman he'd seen earlier, scolding her son for riding his bicycle recklessly.

During the show, the spirits had a message for her: Houdini saw the boy first speeding down a hill, then walking along with his arms hanging limply by his side. The next day, the same boy fell while riding his bicycle and broke his arm. The resulting word-of-mouth publicity guaranteed Houdini a full house for the rest of the week.

After another season with the Welsh Brothers Circus in 1898, the Houdinis were given an endorsement from its management:

> We can cheerfully recommend Harry and Beatrice Houdini with their unique and mysterious act called "Metamorphosis" as being the strongest drawing card of its class in America. Their act is totally unlike others and always creates a profound impression. . . . We will be pleased to play them at any time. The Houdinis are truly great people.[15]

Even with this glowing testimonial, however, the Houdinis barely made a living. But thanks to a fortuitous meeting with a theatrical agent, their fortunes were about to change.

## The Orpheum Circuit

Martin Beck was a short, pudgy German immigrant who had come to America as a singer but had realized he'd do better as an agent. By the time he met Houdini, he had become the head of the powerful Orpheum circuit, one of the biggest chains of vaudeville theaters in the country. He happened to see a performance by Harry and Bess and immediately recognized Houdini's potential.

Beck signed the act up for the entire Orpheum circuit. Houdini was a hit, and by the time he reached California his salary had increased to $90 per week—an all-time high for him and a considerable amount of money for those times.

While he was appearing in San Francisco, the San Francisco *Examiner* ran a story stating that there was nothing miraculous about Houdini's escapes and explaining the use of such typical tricks as a duplicate

*An advertisement for the Houdinis' successful "Metamorphosis" act boasts: "The greatest novelty mystery act in the world."*

key or bent piece of wire. The story was meant to discredit Houdini, but the plan backfired; instead, people talked even more about Houdini. Was it true that he used tricks, or did he have some sort of mysterious power?

Where other, less confident performers might avoid controversy and even

## Challenges

*Walter B. Gibson, in the notes he wrote as editor of* Houdini's Escapes and Magic, *comments about Houdini's innovative challenges to his audience, which the escape artist perfected early in his career.*

"Challenges came under two categories: those where Houdini invited people to bring some standard article, such as a mail bag; and those in which the challengers dared Houdini to attempt an escape from a device of their own construction, such as a brewery barrel. . . .

He could not risk a 'strange' escape unless its condition allowed some opportunity of introducing his familiar methods. As a result, most challenges were planned beforehand. For example, Houdini might agree to escape from a barrel or basket of a certain pattern, even supplying blueprints for the construction of same. This was fair enough from the challenger's standpoint, especially as Houdini frequently called for an object more formidable than the one [the person] would normally supply.

Where the challenger himself came up with an idea, there was always some discussion of the device to be used. Not until the terms were finally agreed upon would the challenge be made public. Usually, the challenge was worded as though the challenger had made it, but comparisons of 'challenges' received by Houdini in various cities show a surprising similarity of ideas. People in one town, however, were unaware of what happened in the next, hence the general conviction was that Houdini was meeting each test for the first time, and this frequently enhanced the performance and enriched the box office as well.

Houdini added to the popular misconception by referring in his publicity to 'freak' escapes, such as his release from a tangle of automobile chains or his escape from the interior of a giant football. These were simply adaptations of his more common escapes, but gave the impression that he could free himself from anything on call."

leave town for good, Houdini did the opposite: he persuaded Beck to organize a repeat date to capitalize on the controversy. He challenged the police to put every restraint they had on him.

After being stripped to the skin at police headquarters and searched by the police surgeon, Houdini allowed them to shackle his hands behind his back, attach leg irons, and fasten ten pairs of handcuffs together to form a chain linking his hand and leg fetters. The police then put him

*A playbill for the Orpheum circuit's vaudeville theater lists Houdini as the headline act.*

in a closet, which had been thoroughly searched beforehand, and closed the door. Ten minutes later, he stepped out of the closet. All the manacles were still locked, but he wasn't in them. Instead, they lay on the floor of the closet.

Then the police enclosed his arms and body with a thick belt used to restrain mental patients. A straitjacket went over this and was padlocked. Again, Houdini was taken to the closet, and again he escaped in a short time. The newspaper ran a retraction of its story and applauded him in print; the resulting publicity, of course, did him a world of good.

The "Naked Test," as it was known, became a regular part of Houdini's publicity antics and was repeated wherever he performed. As one biographer, William Lindsay Gresham, wrote,

> He was fast learning one important fact about the form of showmanship he was making his specialty: it is not what you actually do that counts, but what the public—including the audience in the theater or the reporters at police headquarters—thinks you do.[16]

## Tough Times

Houdini's salary increased to $125 per week after the spectacular demonstration in San Francisco. He was a headliner now, not only on the Orpheum circuit but on the other major vaudeville circuits, such as the Pantages and the Keith. He began advertising his newfound fame in trade journals, to alert bookers who might want to employ him. Houdini was never short on self-confidence. A typical ad might say:

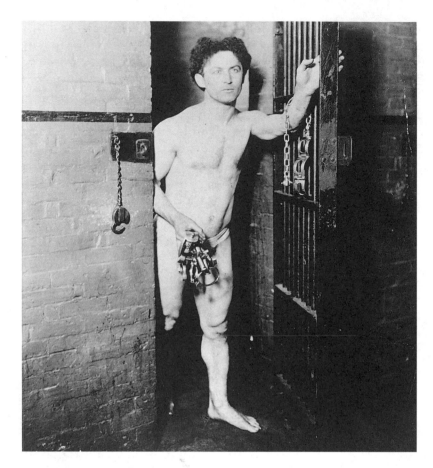

To generate publicity, Houdini created an act called the "Naked Test." After being stripped and searched at police headquarters to make sure he held no keys or tools, Houdini would escape from handcuffs, a straitjacket, and leg irons.

Who created the biggest Sensation in California since the Discovery of Gold in 1849? WHY! HARRY HOUDINI! The ONLY recognized and Undisputed King of Handcuffs and Monarch of Leg Shackles.[17]

Yet despite this relative success, the Houdinis' income was still uncertain, and times were occasionally rough. At home in New York, Houdini advertised that he would give magic lessons. He issued a mail-order catalog that he hoped would generate income:

How to read folded papers in dark rooms, 50 cents. Spirit lock, complete, $2.00. Secret 50 cents. . . . How to cause a hand accordion to give music even though it is tied and sealed up. Secret, 50¢.[18]

Back on the road periodically with Bess as "The Rahners—Sparkling Comedy Team," Houdini would use his off-time to read old humor magazines in barber shops, because it was the cheapest way to come up with material.

The struggling, however, was about to come to an end. When Harry and Bess decided to sail for Europe in 1900, it was the step that would make them international stars.

# 3 Europe and Return

Houdini was a minor figure in American vaudeville when he and his wife left New York for a tour of Europe and Russia at the beginning of the century. By the time they returned home five years later, he was a major international star.

When Harry and Bess sailed in May 1900, they had no bookings lined up. They had only enough money for their steamship passage and a week's room and board once they arrived. Bess had serious misgivings about this risky European venture, but Houdini was optimistic.

He was sure he could find work in European music halls, and he was encouraged by reports from his friend T. Nelson

*Houdini stands on the deck of a steamship headed overseas. His popularity as an entertainer soared after touring Europe and Russia.*

Downs, "the King of Koins," a magician who had become a smash success in London the year before. Houdini's family saw the couple off at the dock, and—except for Houdini's chronic seasickness—it was an uneventful crossing.

## London Failure and Success

Houdini had no luck getting bookings in London, his first stop. He made the rounds of the music halls, handing out

*When Houdini's brash style prohibited him from getting bookings in London, he hired Harry Day (left) to manage his act and secure engagements.*

leaflets, offering to audition, and—in his brash American way—simply telling everyone how great he was. But the theater owners he encountered had the typical British reserve and caution; they ignored this foreigner who tooted his own horn so aggressively.

Houdini's luck began to change, however, when he found a manager. Harry Day, an Englishman who was even younger than Houdini's twenty-six years, had little experience as a manager—but he was enthusiastic and hardworking. Day finally managed to get Houdini a one-week engagement at the Alhambra, London's best vaudeville house.

Houdini's handcuff trick, which now was a major feature of his show, was not entirely new to England; its originator, magician and escape artist Samri Baldwin, had performed it there as early as 1871. But Houdini's twist on it was new—he presented "the challenge," in which he offered to escape from any regulation shackles the audience could provide. Baldwin and other escape artists had always insisted on using their own equipment.

An incident on Houdini's opening night in London created good publicity for the unknown entertainer. As Houdini began his opening-night performance, a rival escape artist named P.H. Cirnoc walked on stage, claiming that Houdini was an impostor and a fraud.

Houdini displayed a huge pair of American-made handcuffs, called Bean Giants after their inventor, and defied Cirnoc to get out of them. Cirnoc refused; he could only escape from his own, specially rigged manacles. Houdini then put the giant cuffs on himself, let Cirnoc fasten them, stepped behind a screen, and emerged a few seconds later free of the cuffs.

## Houdini Issues a Challenge

" £1,000 CHALLENGE OPEN TO THE WORLD

I, HARRY HOUDINI, known as the King of Handcuffs, at last becoming tired of so-called FAKE EXPOSURES and MEDIOCRE MAGICIANS, who claim to DO MY ACT because they possess a lot of false keys and springs, DO HEREBY CHALLENGE any person in the world to duplicate my release from cuffs, irons and straitjackets, under test conditions. That is to entirely strip, be thoroughly searched, mouth SEWED and sealed up, making it impossible to conceal keys, springs, or lock pickers, and in that state escape from all fetters that may be locked or laced on arms, legs or body.

[To] anyone accepting [this] challenge who may, in searching me, find anything concealed on my person, even as small as a pinhead, I forfeit all money wagered, and I have the same rights regarding my opponent. Each competitor is allowed a physician and a mechanic, one to examine the human frame AS ONLY A PHYSICIAN CAN, and the mechanic who will examine all irons used, and if desirable each cuff or fetter can be broken up, so that it may be examined inside as well as out, and prevent faked irons from being used.

Committee shall be selected by mutual consent. No leaving the room to remove fastenings but [this] must be accomplished in the same room behind a newspaper, which is to be used as a curtain, and is to be examined BEFORE AND AFTER using. The place where test is to occur is not to be known by competitors, but must be decided on by committee, SO NO ONE can conceal anything anywhere. Committee is also to be SEARCHED so that they cannot assist the competitors. No less than 12 different styles of IRONS are to be used at one and the same time, also six different makes of Insane Belts, Restraint Maniac Muffs, Canvas and Leather Lace and Lock Straitjackets."

Cirnoc claimed that they had been "gaffed," or rigged for easy escape. Houdini put the irons on Cirnoc, and even gave him the key so that he could open them normally. But Cirnoc couldn't reach the keyhole, because the cuffs were so huge. He didn't know that a special extension to the key was needed. Cirnoc was forced to let Houdini free him, and left the stage in disgrace as the crowd jeered.

The publicity from Cirnoc's failed attempt to discredit Houdini helped him draw audiences all week. The Alhambra's manager then offered Houdini a longer engagement if he could demonstrate on stage the ability to get out of a pair of cuffs from Scotland Yard, the famous detective division of the metropolitan London police.

## Escape from Scotland Yard

Houdini immediately went down to Scotland Yard, accompanied by the theater manager. The police superintendent didn't think much of the brazen young American, but he agreed to wrap Houdini's arms around a pillar and slap a pair of "darbies" (as British handcuffs were called) on him. The superintendent then confidently escorted the theater manager back to his office, telling him that he'd let "the American lad" stay there a while before they returned to let him out.

But Houdini knew that regulation British cuffs could be opened by rapping a certain spot on them against a hard surface. Seconds after the older men had arrived back in the superintendent's office, and much to their astonishment, Houdini was there too.

Houdini got his two weeks' extra booking at the Alhambra and quickly became the talk of London. His engagement at the theater lasted six months, and his weekly salary reached the staggering amount of sixty British pounds (£60). This sum, the equivalent at the time of three hundred U.S. dollars, was much better money than Houdini had ever earned in America.

## On to Germany

Houdini then moved on to Germany and a string of sold-out shows. Sold out, that is, after a brief opening-night scare in Dresden.

Just before show time that evening, the manager of the theater, a man named Kammsetzer, said that if Houdini didn't go over immediately, his run would be canceled. Houdini later wrote:

> You can well imagine my feelings. This manager had brought me to the continent [Europe] with a contract which enabled him to close me right after my first performance if I was not a success, and I was not aware of that fact until just before going on. I was in no mood to do very much talking . . . I had never addressed an audience in German before. I must have said some of the most awful things to make them believe I was good.[19]

In fact, Houdini spoke German well, though with a strong American accent—it was the language he had grown up with. In any event, the night was a triumph. Heavy prison cuffs were put on Houdini, but he escaped from them immediately and, according to the performer's typical-

*An advertisement for a German circus gives Houdini top billing.*

ly enthusiastic account, brought the spectators to their feet:

> When that audience rose in a solid mass . . . I knew I was going to stay my full engagement. And above all the din and noise and shouts and screams of the public, I heard Herr Direktor Kammsetzer's voice shouting like a madman. He ran to the middle of the stage and applauded. He took off his hat and he cheered. In fact, I have no fear of saying that I recorded with him the greatest triumph of any artiste he had ever engaged.[20]

## Success Within a Year

Houdini went on to have a string of successful German engagements. As William Lindsay Gresham notes, Houdini's early appearances in Germany were breathtaking successes:

> Much has been written about Houdini's distinctive act and its implications—the buried wish of Everyman to cast off the shackles of obscurity, poverty, and oppressive restrictions. Perhaps nowhere was this deep appeal more evident than in the Germany of the Kaiser [emperor], where almost everything not compulsory was verboten [forbidden].[21]

In the city of Essen, the huge Krupp armaments (weapons) factory bought out the entire theater so that its employees could see a special performance. That night, Houdini escaped from a set of cuffs that had been specially made for him in the Krupp plant. The act caused so much excitement that Houdini repeated it for the public the next night. The local newspaper, the *Essener Volkszeitung*, said of the occasion:

> Never in the history of the Colosseum Theater have so many persons been contained within its walls as on this memorable night. Not alone was the house sold out, but hundreds were turned away. Contrary to fire and police regulations, the aisles were packed and even the scenery had been removed and chairs were placed on the stage to accommodate the public. Not even the fearful heat could keep away this sweltering mass of humanity and prevent it from giving Houdini an ovation.[22]

Houdini continued to give sold-out performances all across the Continent. His hunch about Europe had worked. A scant year after he had crossed the Atlantic without any prospects or contracts, he had become the strongest vaudeville attraction in Europe.

## The Family Is Reunited

Back in London, Houdini spotted a beautiful dress in a shop window. It had been intended for Queen Victoria, but the British monarch had died before it was finished. Always an impulse buyer, Houdini decided on the spur of the moment that he had to have it for his mother. Houdini bought the dress for £30 ($150), and Bess altered it to fit Cecilia.

Houdini had so many bookings that he knew he wouldn't be back in America soon, and he sensed that his stay in Europe would be a lengthy one. He therefore arranged for his mother's passage to Europe. Since his brother Theo was also an escape artist, Houdini sent him a cable urging him to sail as well: "Come over the apples are ripe."[23]

The night Cecilia Weiss arrived in Hamburg, she proudly watched her son perform before a capacity audience; Houdini had to make special arrangements for an extra seat to be placed in a sold-out box. The next day, the entire family took a train to Budapest. In the finest restaurant in the city, Cecilia, resplendent in her royal gown, presided over a big family reunion.

Houdini remarked later that that day was one of the happiest in his life. As Milbourne Christopher has written:

*Houdini enjoyed huge success as a magician in Europe, giving sold-out performances across the Continent.*

The grandiose gesture was typical of Houdini. As a youngster, he had solemnly promised his father to watch over her; now he fulfilled the vow in superlative fashion. Cecilia sat in a thronelike chair with her son standing by her side and accepted compliments and greetings from relatives she hadn't seen in twenty-seven years.[24]

## The First Loyal Assistant

In Dresden Houdini took on an assistant—the first of what would become a team of skilled workers who were utterly loyal to their boss and his secrets. Franz Kukol, a former officer of the Austrian army, was a tall, distinguished-looking man with an upturned, waxed mustache like the Kaiser's.

One of Kukol's responsibilities was to help Houdini prepare for the stage and then assist him while performing. Another was to take care of the necessary advance work for his boss's arrival in a town. Kukol proved especially useful when Houdini's unorthodox style ran counter to the strict laws typical of German and Prussian governments.

In one German city, Kukol managed to overcome official opposition to Houdini's plan of jumping into the water from a riverbank, loaded down with handcuffs, irons, and chains. Kukol was told by the city officials that no public swimming was allowed; jumping in the water with chains was out of the question.

Nevertheless, Kukol obtained the reluctant permission of the city authorities. On the day of the performance, Houdini jumped in the river and stayed down so long, building up suspense, that the spectators became convinced that he'd drowned. When the escape artist finally bobbed above the water, holding his chains above his head, he was greeted by a wildly cheering crowd. As he walked onto shore, he was also greeted by the local police, who arrested and fined him for walking on the grass!

*Houdini relaxes on a Parisian sidewalk. While in France, Houdini visited the grave of Robert-Houdin and paid homage to his idol with a wreath that read, "Honor and Respect to Robert-Houdin from the Magicians of America."*

## A French Grave Site

While in Paris, Houdini made an effort to visit the widow of Robert-Houdin and pay his respects. He went to her house and asked the maid to announce him, but Madame Robert-Houdin refused to see him. He later found out that the elderly woman had been ill for some years and probably wasn't aware of who her visitor was.

Despite this explanation of the widow's refusal, Houdini was extremely angry at being turned away; he took it as a personal insult. Years later, he wrote a book denouncing Robert-Houdin as a fake. Some biographers suggest that this "insult" from Robert-Houdin's widow marked the beginning of Houdini's change in attitude toward his onetime hero.

Despite his rebuff, Houdini visited Robert-Houdin's grave site in the town of Blois, four hours from Paris by train. Upon learning that the famous magician's daughter lived in the same town, he paid her an unexpected visit before visiting the grave.

The daughter, a sculptor, was busy working in her studio and could not be disturbed. Her husband, however, greeted Houdini cordially, showing him around the house and displaying several clocks that had been made by Robert-Houdin and other memorabilia. He also told Houdini that no one would object if he wanted to visit Robert-Houdin's grave.

Houdini went to the cemetery with a massive wreath that read "Honor and Respect to Robert-Houdin from the Magicians of America." A photographer was present to record the event for the always publicity conscious Houdini. This practice—visiting the graves of famous conjurors, leaving wreaths, and having a photographer memorialize the event—became a lifelong habit for Houdini.

Houdini made a quick business trip to the United States in the spring of 1902. When he returned to Europe after a ten-day stay, he sailed straight into a dramatic courtroom drama.

The trial was the culmination of a suit that had been brought against Houdini some time before. A German police officer named Graff had accused Houdini of not really performing all the escapes he claimed to have accomplished. At the trial, the judges watched as Houdini was put in a regulation German wrist chain—then stared in amazement as Houdini wriggled out of it and dropped it to the floor.

Houdini was found not guilty, and Graff was ordered by the court to apologize publicly. Graff appealed the decision to a higher court, and at that trial provided the escape artist with a special lock, one that had no key. Houdini requested privacy in which to make his escape, was put in a special room, and emerged four minutes later without the shackles.

Houdini again won the decision. Graff took the case to the highest court in Germany—and lost again. The resulting publicity was a gold mine for Houdini, who plastered the Continent wherever he went with posters advertising his victory over "the government of the Kaiser himself."

## Exposing a Fraud

In Germany, Houdini made a detour from his regular scheduled shows to vindicate his honor. A rival escape artist, Kleppini, was appearing in the town of Essen, falsely

## A Change of Heart

*Psychoanalyst Bernard C. Meyer, in* Houdini: A Mind in Chains, *reflects on Houdini's sudden change of heart about his onetime idol, Robert-Houdin.*

"Surely it was no accident that the first signs of the repudiation of his idol coincided with the beginnings of his European success. Standing on the threshold of personal glory, in the full gaze of his adoring mother and exulting in the drama of her 'enthronement,' Houdini must have believed that at last his hour had come: the 'son' had become the equal of the 'father,' and the moment had arrived when he might uncoil and strike.

In seeking to account for this *volte-face* [about-face], it should be noted that the publication of *The Unmasking of Robert-Houdin* [Houdini's book about the magician] was not to be the only blast he would fire at someone he had once loved or esteemed. Some ten years after the publication of this work, he was to repeat that performance in the treatment of his younger brother, Dr. Leopold Weiss, who, allegedly for having married the divorced wife of an older brother, became the hated object of Houdini's undying wrath."

claiming that he'd won a handcuff duel with Houdini. In fact, the two had never met.

Houdini changed his hairstyle, donned a false mustache, and sat in the audience at Kleppini's show, which was part of a circus. Kleppini started his show by boasting of his victory over Houdini.

Suddenly, an old man in the audience jumped up to say, "Not true, not true!"

"How do you know?" Kleppini replied.

The old man said simply, "I know, I know." He leaped onto the stage and ripped off his mustache. It was Houdini.

Houdini then challenged Kleppini to a duel at a later date using a set of French "letter cuffs." These handcuffs would open only when a set of five cylinders had been spun to spell out a predetermined word.

The night before the duel, Houdini leaked some information to the business manager of Kleppini's circus: the word to open the cuffs would be CLEFS, French for "keys." Before a capacity crowd the next night, Kleppini asked to see the cuffs and quickly darted behind a screen, obviously checking to see if CLEFS was still the right word.

He wanted to put the shackles on immediately, but Houdini insisted that he wait. The two men shoved each other around the stage while arguing. Finally, Houdini agreed and closed the cuffs around Kleppini's wrists.

Kleppini confidently entered the cabinet, and Houdini made an announcement:

> Ladies and gentlemen, you can all go home. I do not lock a cuff on a man merely to let him escape. If he tries this cuff until doomsday, he cannot open it. To prove this, though the regular closing time of the circus is ten thirty, I will allow him to remain here until two thirty.[25]

Kleppini had entered the cabinet at nine P.M. Half an hour later, he had made no progress. The cabinet was moved aside so that the rest of the circus could continue. By eleven, most of the audience had gone home and the manager called a halt.

Kleppini ran to the manager's office and continued his efforts while Houdini stood guard.

Finally, at one A.M., the manager ordered Kleppini to stop. In the presence of the manager and a reporter, Houdini spun the cylinders to release him. The word that opened the cuffs was FRAUD. During the on-stage struggle, Houdini had switched the combination.

## Psyching Out the Audience

Often, Houdini relied on sheer physical strength and skill to make his escapes, and sometimes the challenges were genuinely

*Houdini used sheer strength and agility to make his escapes. He relied equally on his great showmanship to maximize the drama of his performances.*

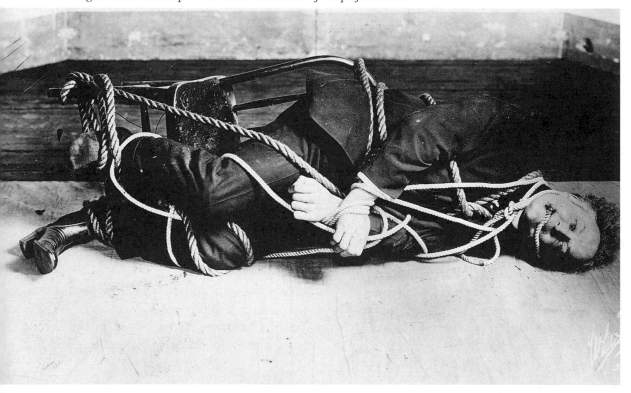

## Houdini on Showmanship

Houdini on Magic, *a collection of the performer's writings edited by Walter B. Gibson and Morris N. Young, reprints a newspaper piece by Houdini called "Addressing an Audience." It outlines some of Houdini's own philosophy regarding showmanship, which he developed early in his career.*

"The great trouble with magicians is the fact that they believe when they have bought a certain trick or piece of apparatus, and know the method of procedure, that they are full-fledged mystifiers. The fact really is, it is not the trick itself, nor is it the mere handling of it. A successful presentation depends on the address in connection with the presentation. . . .

My method of addressing an audience as result of experience was as follows: I would walk down to the footlights, actually put one foot over the electric globes as if I were going to spring among the people, and then hurl my voice saying, 'Ladies and Gentlemen'. . . .

When you introduce an experiment, apply yourself seriously. Don't think that because you perform a trick well or the apparatus is detection proof from the viewpoint of an ordinary audience, that you have conquered the world of mystery and that you reign supreme. Work with determination that you intend to make them *believe* what you say. Say it as if you mean it, and believe it yourself. If you *believe* your own claim to miracle doing and are sincere in your work, you are bound to succeed."

difficult. Sometimes, though, Houdini relied just as heavily on his ability to pump up an audience psychologically to fever pitch.

Typical was his escape from a bank vault on stage. Houdini, wearing only bathing trunks, would first be inspected by a doctor to make sure he was not hiding anything. Also on hand, however, would be a "referee" from the audience—who was, in fact, Houdini's friend, the British magician Will Goldston. To the average observer, Goldston, tall and balding, with glasses and a proper hat, was every inch the respectable London banker. The audience never suspected that this upstanding-looking man passed Houdini a specially made tool as they shook hands before Houdini entered the vault.

The vault was then moved behind a screen. Escaping from it took Houdini only a moment, but he would deliberately lounge around behind the screen, reading a book, for nearly an hour. Meanwhile, the audience, which was listening to the theater orchestra play, was slowly going mad with tension. At the last moment, Houdini would muss up his hair, step out from behind the screen while pretending he was exhausted, and drink in the applause.

Houdini had been a professional performer since his teens, and had learned well the single most important secret of magic: how to misdirect the audience's attention. He began to imply, in interviews and advertising, that he possessed a secret—that his escapes relied not on a number of explainable methods but on a single, mystical secret. As Milbourne Christopher notes, the strategy brilliantly fooled Houdini's audience: "This was the most artistic kind of misdirection, for almost everything he did depended on a different principle."[26]

In 1904 Houdini made a spectacular escape on a London stage from a one-of-a-kind set of handcuffs. A master locksmith from Birmingham had labored five years to make them, and they were advertised as the strongest ever built: there were six sets of locks and nine tumblers in each cuff.

The show, at London's Hippodrome, drew a capacity crowd of four thousand. Houdini appeared onstage in his usual black cutaway coat, striped trousers, gray vest, gray ascot tie, and stiff wing collar. He allowed the cuffs to be placed on him and then made a speech:

> *Ladies and gentlemen*: I am now locked up in a handcuff that has taken a British mechanic five years to make. I do not know whether I am going to get out of it or not, but I can assure you I am going to do my best.[27]

Houdini then entered the small cloth-covered cabinet as forty audience members surrounded it. Twenty-two minutes later, he came out—but he was still shackled. He wanted to ask for more light.

The lights were turned up, and the orchestra struck up another tune. Thirty-five minutes later, Houdini, who was kneeling inside the cabinet, announced that his knees were sore. He was provided with a cushion. Another twenty minutes passed, and a sweating Houdini emerged from the cabinet to ask that the cuffs be removed so that he could take off his coat.

He was told by representatives of the newspaper that had sponsored the contest, the London *Daily Mirror*, that to do so would be to admit defeat. Houdini then removed his coat himself: he twisted his hands around until he could reach his vest pocket, took out a penknife, and opened it with his teeth. He then yanked the coat over his head and off his arms, so that it was dangling by his hands. Holding the knife in his teeth, Houdini sliced open the coat until it fell off him.

The audience roared its approval of this bold act, and Houdini went back inside his cabinet. Finally, an hour and ten minutes after starting, he leaped from the cabinet. His hands were free and he was holding the cuffs aloft in triumph. The crowd stormed the stage and carried a visibly exhausted Houdini on its shoulders into the streets and on to his hotel.

## On to Imperial Russia

In 1903 Houdini traveled to Russia to continue his string of spectacular performances. Russia then was a monarchy, ruled by an emperor, Czar Nicholas Romanov and his family; the Russian Revolution was more than a decade away.

Houdini got into trouble early during his stay. He was in the habit of practicing his stage patter—especially if it was in a new language—out loud in public places such as parks. One day, he was bellowing in his phonetically learned Russian at the top of his lungs in a Moscow park when he was carted off by the police, who thought he was a madman. He was rescued from jail by Bess, who convinced the police that Houdini wasn't a lunatic.

The mix-up with the authorities eventually proved to be fortuitous. Because of it, Houdini made the acquaintance of the chief of Russia's secret police, who was persuaded to let the escape artist try his hand with a type of carriage known as a Siberia wagon.

The Siberia wagon, so called because it was used for the three-week journey to transport convicts to that remote part of Russia, was a fearsome affair. Designed to be pulled by horses, it was strongly built, with a single door in back that could be securely padlocked. The only window was eight inches square, set in the door and crossed by iron bars. There were no holes anywhere in the walls, which were made of wood covered with solid sheet steel. Inside, the walls were lined with sheets of zinc.

Houdini escaped from this formidable trap in exactly twenty-eight minutes. The most widely held theory as to how he did it—the one Houdini liked to tell—is that he secreted a cutting tool on his person, sawed through the zinc floor and wooden floorboards, and peeled the zinc floor back enough to get out. A more likely explanation is that he was simply able to reach a hand through the window and pick the outside padlock. (The posters that Houdini later had made to publicize the event show the wagon having a much smaller window, placed higher up on the door, than it really was.)

The Russian authorities, Houdini later claimed, refused to sign a document attesting to his successful escape. They were embarrassed enough, he said, that his escape from a wagon designed to transport desperate criminals for three weeks at a stretch had taken less than half an hour. The police didn't need the extra humiliation of having that escape announced publicly.

## Home to America

On a return visit to America in 1904, Houdini contracted pneumonia and was forced to take a rare rest from his backbreaking

*Twenty years after Houdini joined the Society of American Magicians, his picture graces the program for their annual dinner.*

schedule. While recuperating in New York, he was inducted into the Society of American Magicians (SAM), a fraternal organization in which he would play an important role in years to come.

He also used some of the money he'd earned in Europe to buy a house, a four-story brownstone building at 278 West 113th Street in Manhattan. It cost him $25,000—a fortune at the time. The house, which would be his headquarters until he died, had twenty-six rooms—plenty of space for Cecilia and for himself and Bess, as well as for his rapidly growing collection of rare books on magic, posters, apparatus bought from famous magicians, and other memorabilia.

"The finest private house that any magician has ever had the great fortune to possess," Houdini called it,[28] forgetting in his enthusiasm such palatial estates owned by magicians as the lavish Long Island house of Herrman the Great, Robert-Houdin's chateau in St. Gervais, or Mellini's mansion in Hanover.

On this trip, Houdini also bought a large plot at Machpelah Cemetery, a Jewish burial ground in Cypress Hills, Long Island. He then had the bodies of his father and his half-brother Herman transferred there. In his private journal, Houdini made the odd notation that "Herman's teeth were in splendid condition."[29]

Houdini was now the premier vaudeville attraction in Europe, but he had yet to crack the American market. He was determined now to make himself a star in his own country.

# 4 From Magician to Escape Artist

The year 1905, when Houdini began concentrating on adding American audiences to the European audiences he'd already conquered, was a turning point. It marked the final transition from his earliest beginnings—as a more or less standard magician and entertainer—to the mature image by which he became famous as the king of escape artists.

During the next decade, Houdini introduced increasingly difficult and inventive traps, including some of his best-known stunts, such as the escape from a milk can or water can and the Chinese torture cell escape. He performed some of his most spectacular feats of magic, including the famous disappearing elephant. He toured ceaselessly and made his name familiar the world over. And he also experienced a personal tragedy from which he would never fully recover—the death of his beloved mother.

*Houdini prepares for a straitjacket escape. Such difficult feats heightened his popularity in the United States and earned him the title of king of escape artists.*

## Assault on America

With his skills sharpened by the years of steady work in Europe, Houdini mounted an all-out publicity campaign to ensure success when he opened in America. Never one for false modesty, Houdini hammered away at booking agents and public alike about his own greatness. Typical of this brashness is this ad, which appeared in large type in a New York theatrical paper at Christmas 1905, when other promotions were full of gentle Yuletide cheer:

I TOLD YOU SO!!!

WHEN IT WAS DISCOVERED THAT HOUDINI, "THE PRISON DEFIER," HAD BEEN BROUGHT BACK TO AMERICA AT A SALARY OF $1,000 WEEKLY, ALL THE WISEENHEIMERS [smart alecks] AND SOCIETY OF KNOW-IT-ALL FELLOWS POLISHED UP THEIR HAMMERS, SAYING, "GOLD BRICK!"

IT HAS NOW BEEN POSITIVELY PROVEN BEYOND ANY CONTRADICTION THAT HOUDINI IS THE HARDEST WORKING ARTIST THAT

---

### A Terrible Review

*Although Houdini was generally well received when he returned to America, not everyone was impressed. This review, by critic Alan Dale in the New York* American, *is quoted in Milbourne Christopher's* Houdini: The Untold Story.

"The 'famous' Houdini is a clever manipulator of handcuffs who appears to suffer in the very worst way from that terrible and baffling disease—the swollen head. Houdini devoted the greater part of his 'turn' [act] to talking about himself in a cheap and rather pitiful way. It was all as dull as ditch water. A good deal of his poor talk was 'gallery play'—what a hard time he had of it in England, how they hated to see him earning money over there, how cruelly jealous they were of him in Blackburn, but that he'd go back there and get more money. If he doesn't do a better turn in Blackburn than he did here in Harlem, I don't fancy that he'll succeed in his design of 'getting more money.' This was all piffle and sad piffle.

Years ago I saw this really clever young man in London and was delighted with what I saw, but now it all seems spoiled. Even the particularly effective trick in which Houdini is apparently padlocked into a huge can of water, from which he successfully 'emerges' in his cabinet, is marred by the offensive manners of the man."

HAS EVER TRODDEN THE VAUDE-
VILLE STAGE!!!

HE IS WORTH MORE THAN
THE SALARY HE IS BOOKED
FOR!!![30]

Houdini also publicized himself by ex-
ploiting his knack for escaping from jail
cells, hitting pay dirt when he escaped
from cell #2 of the South Wing of the U.S.
Jail in Washington, D.C. This cell was famous because it had been used to detain
Charles J. Guiteau prior to his execution
for the assassination of President James A.
Garfield in 1881.

*Always looking for new ways to promote himself,
Houdini exploited his ability to escape from jail cells.*

Houdini was stripped and searched
before being locked in the cell, but was
out within two minutes; he then opened
the other cells and moved convicts around
to different cells. Shocked by the appearance of a naked man in the jail, the inmates sheepishly obeyed. One man,
serving time for manslaughter, meekly
asked Houdini, "Have you come to let me
out? What are you doing without
clothes?"[31] At least, that's how Houdini re-
ported it later.

When he was done, Houdini dressed
and walked to the warden's office, where
newspaper reporters waited. Less than half
an hour had elapsed since Houdini had
been placed in his cell.

Houdini reaped massive publicity
from this stunt and also blocked future rivals from imitating him. He did this by
having the warden sign a statement saying:

> The experiment was a valuable one in
> that the department has been instruct-
> ed as to the adoption of further securi-
> ty which will protect any lock from
> being opened or interfered with.[32]

Houdini had a number of methods to
help in his escapes. Sometimes a prison
would be visited by Houdini or a confeder-
ate before the escape, during which time
an impression of a key could be made or
tools dropped in a crack in the floor.

Also, Houdini took advantage of the
fact that prison doctors of the time often
wore coats made of heavy black broad-
cloth. He carried with him a tiny toolbag
made of this material and equipped with a
hook. He'd hook the bag on the doctor's
back before being examined by the physician. When the examination was over,
Houdini would clap the doctor heartily on
the back and retrieve his bag.

*Hands cuffed and body shackled, Houdini bewilders his audience by escaping his formidable restraints.*

In Boston, Houdini caused a sensation when he broke out of a maximum-security cell and entered another, where his clothes were stored. He dressed, climbed the prison wall, and ran through the snow to the theater where he was appearing. He then placed a telephone call to the prison superintendent, who was waiting patiently in his office at the penitentiary.

One of Houdini's many books and pamphlets came from this period. It was called *The Right Way to Do Wrong*, and it revealed in detail the most common professional techniques of burglars, pickpockets, safecrackers, and other criminals. Houdini's books were popular in their time but have long since gone out of print.

## Escape from an Underwater Packing Crate

Another way in which Houdini made the headlines was by being handcuffed and nailed inside a packing crate, which was tossed into a river.

For this escape, Houdini relied on his strength and stamina; he even had an oversized bathtub installed in his house, so that he could practice holding his breath for long periods. But he also relied on his assistants' skills at "gaffing" the mechanism.

Although it looked normal to the inspecting committees, one board of the crate had concealed hinges and catches. The lid seemed to be tight, but the screws had been shortened so that they could be pushed out from inside. Houdini could get out quickly, but he routinely heightened the suspense by staying underwater until his breath was gone—long past the time most observers thought he was surely dead.

When Houdini opened at Hammerstein's Roof Garden theater in New York, a central part of his nightly show was a re-creation of this stunt in a huge tank of water. By this time, Houdini was a top draw and was making the enormous sum of $1,000 a week.

Houdini claimed later that he demanded his first week's pay in gold pieces, which he presented to his mother by saying, "Mamma—do you remember before Father died, he made me promise to always take care of you? . . . Hold out your apron!" And he poured the gold coins into her apron. Houdini said that the experience was the happiest moment of his life.[33]

## Friends and Enemies

Houdini's personality was moody and volatile, and he formed strong likes and dislikes quickly. One person he had never become friendly with was Bess's mother, Mrs. Rahner, who still vigorously opposed her daughter's marriage to a Jew.

But when Bess became ill one winter, Houdini went to Mrs. Rahner's house and demanded that she come to her daughter's bedside so that the two could be reconciled. Through Houdini's force of will, Bess's mother complied. Eventually, Mrs. Rahner warmed up to Houdini—he later bought her a piano and other gifts—and she even became close with Houdini's mother, Cecilia.

In many ways Houdini was intensely jealous of other magicians and protective about his own secrets. But he also revealed some of these secrets in articles in *Conjuror's Monthly*, a magazine that he started, and in his books. This may seem

*One of Houdini's most memorable escapes involved being handcuffed and placed into a packing crate which was then nailed shut and lowered into the water. He stunned observers by surviving this death-defying act.*

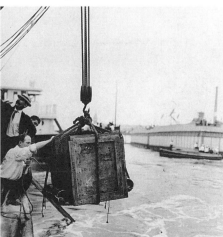

## The Master Showman

*Walter B. Gibson, in his editorial notes for* Houdini's Escapes and Magic, *comments on Houdini's growing mastery of showmanship as he matured.*

"The greatest factor in Houdini's success was his showmanship. He knew how to present his escapes so that they were both amazing and spectacular; and with his ability as a showman he also possessed a thorough knowledge of every form or type of escape.

He was familiar with every type of lock and every make of handcuff. He was constantly experimenting and inventing new tools and appliances. His natural ingenuity and long experience gave him full confidence in his ability to meet any challenge or to attempt any form of escape.

Houdini could employ a regular escape, using a method well known among escape artists, and present it with the same effectiveness that marked the other items in his program. On the contrary, there were escapes in Houdini's repertoire that could not have been successfully accomplished by his imitators even if he had given them the instructions."

*Houdini adds a new twist to his straitjacket escape by performing it upside down.*

surprising, since his career depended on the exclusivity of his methods. But he hoped to discourage imitators by giving away the more common secrets of their trade, while keeping his own innovations to himself.

Houdini also wrote extensively in his magazine about one of his great loves, the history of magic. Walter B. Gibson, who edited Houdini's writings after his death, notes:

> He presented the details in a homely, direct way with pointed sidelights that give considerable perspective to the "history makers" as Houdini styled the old-time magicians whose lives he chronicled. . . . Houdini deserves more credit for this work than any of his other contributions to the field of magic.[34]

## A Variety of Stunts and One-of-a-Kind Events

During this period, Houdini redoubled his efforts to come up with new and exciting escapes. Many of these were one-of-a-kind events such as having the entire University of Pennsylvania football team, in uniform, jog down a theater aisle carrying a giant football. Upon mounting the stage, the team worked together to manacle Houdini, then put him inside the football and laced it shut with a brass chain and a padlock. Houdini was out in thirty-five minutes.

Others became standard items in his shows. In one famous escape, for example, a shackled Houdini was lowered into an oversized milk can filled with water. When he was completely immersed, the lid was

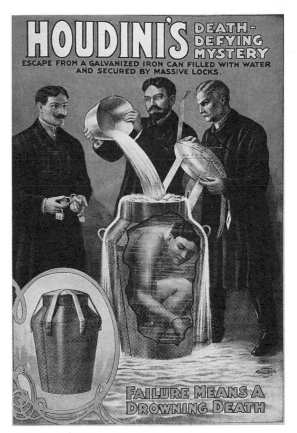

*A poster publicizes Houdini's escape from an oversized milk can filled with water, a stunt that became a standard act in his shows.*

bolted on tight and a curtained screen put up between him and the audience.

Houdini would have his audiences hold their breaths as he went into the can, confident that they would all be gasping and wheezing long before he emerged. Meanwhile, the band in the orchestra pit played a song called "Asleep in the Deep," which contains the words: "Many brave hearts are asleep in the deep—sailor, beware; sailor, take care."

Although it took Houdini only about three minutes to escape from the can, thanks to the way his assistants had rigged it, he would sometimes stay behind the

ready to break open the can and rescue him if needed. In fact, they were never needed—their presence merely added to the thrill.

## Still More Escapes

Houdini was always wary of slipping out of the public eye. If he didn't keep coming up with exciting new material, he'd suffer the ultimate insult—to be second on the bill. To ensure repeat business, he always made sure that his audiences knew about any new material he planned to do later in the week.

He jumped into rivers with a 75-pound iron ball attached to his foot. He escaped from "wet packs"—cocoons of wet bedsheets wrapped around the body, which were used to restrain violent patients in mental institutions. He escaped from ladders to which he had been lashed by groups of sailors. He got out of a giant cardboard box without tearing the box.

Sometimes his escapes genuinely took a long time to complete—never mind the suspense-building psychology. In Toledo, Ohio, it took him forty-one minutes to get free of some tarred ropes; in the same city, he spent an hour and twenty minutes escaping from a boiler secured with steel bars. These were real challenges that did not provide an opportunity to "gaff" the mechanism.

Audiences today would be hard put to wait for their thrills as long as Houdini's audiences did. Spending half an hour or an hour listening to a band, with nothing to look at onstage but a curtained screen, would try a modern theatergoer's patience to the limit.

*To keep his name in the spotlight, Houdini untiringly experimented with a variety of escapes, always searching for exciting new material to add to his shows.*

curtain for up to half an hour. Audiences would become increasingly agitated, thinking that he was surely in danger. Houdini added to their anxieties by having his assistants stand by with fire axes,

But Houdini's knack for building suspense—as well as a greater willingness on the part of audiences to wait patiently— saw him through. The evidence indicates that audiences in smaller towns were especially willing to wait through long periods of inactivity. As biographer William Lindsay Gresham remarks, "in the Middle West, audiences seemed limitless in their patience."[35]

## Practice

In both his writing and performances, Houdini stressed the importance of constant practice to maintain mental and physical agility. He kept in shape by performing complex card or coin manipulations, without looking, while reading or talking with friends.

Houdini felt that this was key to success for any performer. According to Kellock in *Houdini: His Life Story*, Houdini remarked that his most important secret was

> vigorous self-training, to enable me to do remarkable things with my body, to make not one muscle or a group of muscles, but *every* muscle, a responsive worker, quick and sure for its part, to make my fingers super-fingers in dexterity, and to train my toes to do the work of fingers.[36]

Houdini practiced anywhere, anytime. While relaxing at home, he would tie and untie knots in a length of rope with his feet while conversing with friends or family. He even practiced while eating; in his book *Handcuff Secrets* he wrote:

> The primary lesson is, to learn to use both hands with equal facility. . . . The

method adopted by me to acquire this end was, when at table I practiced to use the left hand persistently, until I could use it almost as easily as the right.[37]

Constant practice, he felt, ensured self-confidence. He considered self-confidence absolutely essential, especially when one was presenting an already familiar act. "Don't lose confidence in an effect because it has been presented many times before," he wrote in an article reprinted in *Houdini's Escapes and Magic:*

> An old trick in "good hands" is always new. Just see to it that yours are "good hands." Don't allow yourself to "go stale" on your act. Keep up your enthusiasm! There is nothing more contagious than exuberant enthusiasm, and it is sure to "get" an audience.[38]

## Ego Problems

Houdini was supremely self-confident in many ways; in others, he was painfully insecure. An incident that occurred in 1908 is indicative of how easily Houdini's feelings could be hurt and his ego bruised. Houdini was elected vice president of the Society of American Magicians, but resigned only a few weeks later. The reason had to do with the society's yearbook.

Some years before, while in Dresden, Germany, Houdini had visited the grave of the great magician Bosco. The grave was sadly neglected and in disrepair, so Houdini bought the plot and arranged for its perennial maintenance with the compliments of SAM. The society's yearbook for 1908 said only that "a member" had done

## Straitjackets

*In an article reprinted in* Houdini's Escapes and Magic *edited by Walter B. Gibson, Houdini explained how a strong, agile person could escape from a straitjacket.*

"It [the jacket] is made of strong brown canvas or sail cloth and has a deep leather collar and leather cuffs; these cuffs are sewn up at the ends, making a sort of bag into which each arm is placed; the seams are covered with leather bands, attached to which are leather straps and steel buckles which, when strapped upon a person, fit and buckle up in back.

The sleeves of this jacket are made so long that when the arms of the wearer are placed in them and folded across the chest, the leather cuffs of the sleeves, to which are attached straps and buckles, meet at the back of the body, one overlapping the other. The opening of the straitjacket is at the back, where several straps and buckles are sewn which are fastened at the back.

The first step necessary to free yourself is to place the elbow, which has the continuous hand *under* the opposite elbow, on some solid foundation and by sheer strength exert sufficient force at this elbow so as to force it gradually up towards the head, and by further persistent straining you can eventually force the head under the *lower arm*, which results in bringing both of the encased arms in front of the body.

Once having freed your arms to such an extent as to get them in front of the body, you can now undo the buckles of the straps of the cuffs with your teeth, after which you open the buckles at the back with your hands, which are still encased in the canvas sleeves, and then you remove the straitjacket from your body."

this good deed, without mentioning Houdini by name. Houdini was offended by this omission and used it as his reason for resigning.

A few years later, however, Houdini would help found another organization, the Magicians' Club, in London. He personally paid the first six months' rent on the club's quarters and was elected its first president. He also later patched up his quarrel with SAM, becoming its national president in 1917.

As he aged, he seemed to mellow toward other magicians, seeing them more as friends and colleagues than as rivals out to steal his ideas. Age did not dim his ego, however. A Baltimore magician named Arthur Gans once went backstage to greet his friend Houdini between shows. Gans was warmly welcomed to Houdini's dressing room, but he then tried to introduce a companion by saying, "And this is our Maryland escape king." Houdini icily replied, "I recognize no other escape kings," and walked out of the dressing room.

His ego was strong in other ways, too. Although he and Bess never had children, Houdini was generally friendly toward boys who emulated him—as long as they did not try to do escape tricks or ruffle his image as a superman. And he continued to be sensitive about his height; he had a specially carved chair for himself to sit in during meetings of the London Magicians' Club, to ensure that his head was above everyone else's.

## Traveling with "the Boys"

In 1909 Houdini hired two new assistants, Englishmen named Jim Collins and Jim Vickery. Collins, a red-haired master mechanic and cabinetmaker, would become especially valuable to Houdini. The troupe traveled in two railcars; one carried baggage, props, and a portable library designed by Collins to hold one hundred books. The other had three rooms—one for Harry and Bess, one for "the boys," and one that Collins used as a workshop for cutting keys and making other gimmicks.

Houdini was a stern taskmaster, and his volatile temper kept everyone on their toes. If one of "the boys" made a mistake, Houdini would instantly fire him and then become indignant if the man took the firing seriously, since it suggested disloyalty. Houdini fired Collins once a week on general principles, because the Englishman so seldom made mistakes that there was rarely a genuine reason to fire him.

"It was an exciting, exhausting life," writes William Lindsay Gresham of this period. "When Jim heard the Boss screaming, 'Collins! Collins! Get in here quick!' he never knew whether he had mislaid a handcuff key, whether the theater was on fire, or whether Houdini had just had a revolutionary new idea. . . ."[39]

## Houdini Down Under

Early in 1910, Harry and his entourage sailed to Australia for a tour. He was paid very well, including two months' salary for the time spent sailing to and from Australia. Otherwise, such a long journey would not have been worth the desperate seasickness he had predictably endured. When Houdini's ship finally docked in Adelaide, he began eating huge meals to put on the twenty-five pounds he'd lost during the crossing.

The promoter Harry Rickards gave Houdini a Barnum-like buildup in the land Down Under. A typical advertising flyer ran: "The Talk of the Town in Train, Tram and Taxi. Absolutely the Greatest and most Sensational Act that has ever been engaged by any Manager."[40]

The four-week tour of Australia was a solid, if not spectacular, success; it seems the Australian audiences were too impatient to sit for half an hour while Houdini labored to get out of his restraints. Another chapter in the Houdini legend was born, however, when, according to the reports in the Australian newspapers, Houdini jumped from a bridge with such force that a corpse was dislodged from the river bottom and floated to the surface.

## In the Air

Houdini's real achievement in Australia was not in performing, but in becoming the first person to successfully fly an airplane there.

The year before, in Germany, Houdini had seen an airplane for the first time and had immediately fallen in love. He had bought a French-made biplane, painted HOUDINI in big letters on the machine's rudder, and hired a mechanic to teach him to fly. Both plane and mechanic came with him to Australia.

Houdini was obsessed with his new love. He even learned to drive a car, just so that he could get out to the airfield early in the morning. By all accounts, though, he was a terrible driver. No one but the mechanic would ride with him.

*The ever fearless Houdini became the first person to successfully fly an airplane to Australia. Though he was initially obsessed with flying, oddly, he never flew again after this feat.*

In Melbourne, where Houdini was appearing, strong winds kept him from attempting a flight for several weeks. When the winds died down, he took off and successfully flew for nearly a mile at fifty miles an hour—quite an achievement for the time, less than seven years after the historic flights of the Wright brothers.

To mark the occasion, Houdini was presented with a trophy by a group of Sydney flying enthusiasts. It was inscribed: "The Aerial League of Australia to H. Houdini for the First Aerial Flight in Australia, March 16, 1910."[41]

After he left Australia, Houdini never flew a plane or drove a car again. As biographer William Lindsay Gresham wrote, "His passion died down as quickly as it had arisen."[42]

## Guns, Alcohol, and Brick Walls

Back in England, Houdini was challenged by four officers of the Chatham Naval Barracks. Their letter read:

> We CHALLENGE you to stand in front of a loaded Government 8-cwt. [800-pound] Steel Gun, to which we will secure you, insert a fuse which will burn 20 minutes, and if you fail to release yourself within that time you will be blown to Kingdom Come.[43]

The challenge was accepted, but the local chief of police objected for safety reasons. Finally, a compromise was reached: the navy men could load the gun, but they could not light the fuse. Onstage, the officers secured Houdini to the gun muzzle with ropes and tied him up tightly.

There was no screen between Houdini and his audience, so they were able to watch his every move. He kicked off his shoes and, with his bare toes, untied the knots binding his hands. Then he wriggled out of all the other restraints, finishing with three minutes to spare.

In Leeds, Houdini agreed to be sealed into his water can as usual—except that the can was to be filled with beer. Houdini, who never drank, was overcome by the alcohol. Kukol was finally forced to pull him out of the can. It was a rare downfall for Houdini.

Afterward, a stagehand said, "Why run away from the beer, Mr. Houdini? It's what most of us run after."[44] But Houdini was not amused; he hated to admit defeat. Later, he figured out how to successfully perform the escape—by coating his body with oil so that the alcohol would not affect him.

In another stunt, Houdini apparently walked through a solid brick wall. This illusion had been performed by the Great Alexander years before Houdini picked it up, but he perfected and popularized it.

First, a wide rug was spread on stage. A larger sheet of seamless muslin was laid over it. Each floor covering was examined by a committee from the audience, to ensure that there were no holes or tears in the material. Meanwhile, a squad of bricklayers built a wall on a steel beam that was one foot wide and ten feet long, mounted on rolling casters three inches from the floor. They made the wall eight feet high.

The committee was placed around the wall, their feet firmly on the muslin. Screens were arranged to shield Houdini from view. Houdini would wave one hand at the audience above the screen—and then, a few moments later, would wave again, this time on the other side of the brick wall.

There was no way he could have gone under the steel beam, because it was only a few inches off the ground, or around the sides, because they were blocked by committee members. By all appearances, he had simply melted through the wall.

In fact, there was a trap door underneath the rug and below the wall. When it was opened, Houdini had just enough space to wriggle underneath it, between the rug and the steel beam. The weight of the committee members kept the rug from sinking too far.

## His Mother Dies

In July 1913, following an American tour, Houdini stood on the deck of his sailing ship, reluctantly saying goodbye to his beloved mother as he prepared to sail again for Europe.

Cecilia was seventy-two years old and in frail health. Harry asked her what she wanted as a souvenir from abroad, but all she could think of was a certain type of woolen slippers, size six, that she particularly liked.

When Houdini finally said goodbye—he was the last one up the gangplank because he couldn't stop embracing his mother—Cecilia returned to the house on West 113th Street. There, she performed a familiar ritual: she wound the grandfather clock that Houdini himself always took care of when he was in town.

A few days later, Theo took Cecilia for a vacation to Asbury Park, New Jersey, where he was opening at the Lyric Theater. On July 14, she suffered a stroke at her hotel. Theo immediately sent Houdini

a cable, but the escape artist had not yet landed in Europe. Their sister Gladys arrived in Asbury Park from New York the next morning, and Cecilia died on the evening of July 16.

When Harry finally reached Copenhagen and got the cable from Theo, he was devastated. Reports on the exact chain of events vary; some accounts say Houdini immediately canceled all his appearances and sailed on the next ship home, leaving Jim Collins to deal with the broken contract. Such disregard of a written agreement was a serious offense in Denmark at the time, and Collins apparently was jailed briefly. After he had explained the matter to the theater manager, however, the executive compassionately allowed Houdini to break the contract.

Another report states that Houdini received the cable announcing his mother's death during a press conference in Copenhagen. According to this story, he opened the cable, read it, and fell unconscious to the floor. When he came to, he sobbed, "Mother—my dear little mother—poor little mama." The reporters quietly left the room.[45]

In any event, Houdini did sail home immediately. While in port in Bremen on the way back to New York, he bought a pair of warm woolen slippers. He placed them in Cecilia's coffin when she was buried, on July 30, in the Machpelah Cemetery plot, next to her husband.

## A Period of Grief

For weeks afterward, Houdini spent almost every day at his mother's graveside. Sometimes he would lie down on top of

*Houdini and Bess visit Houdini's mother's grave site. Houdini never stopped mourning the loss of his beloved mother.*

her grave, face down, and talk to her. He had her letters to himself, dating back to 1900, translated into English and typed up, so that he could read and reread them more easily. He stopped the grandfather clock that had once been her responsibility to wind. His personal stationery now carried a wide black border. He spent much of his time writing prose poems to his mother, which he had printed at his own expense.

He was able to begin work again in September, when he returned to Europe to honor engagements there. Houdini continued some of his activities in his usual vigorous way, such as adding to his growing collection of magicians' memorabilia and starting a fund to maintain the grave of a famous Scottish magician, John Henry Anderson.

But Harry's period of mourning really lasted for the rest of his life. Everyone who was close to Houdini agreed that something seemed to have gone out of him and

his show—that he seemed listless and uninspired. He could have been booked solidly through the winter, but he was too depressed to work full time.

His mother was always on his mind. At a Magicians' Club supper in London, held in his honor shortly after Cecilia's death, Houdini made a speech that summed up his feelings:

My mother was everything to me. It seemed like the end of the world when she was taken from me. Not until she lay dying did I realize how inexpressibly futile is a man's intelligence and determination when face to face with death. When her last hour came, I thought mine would soon follow. Everything seemed turned to dust and ashes for me. All desire for fame and fortune had gone from me. I was alone with my bitter agony. But time, the great healer, has brought me some measure of solace.[46]

# 5 Magic and Movies: During and After the War

Houdini generally had little interest in world affairs, but World War I, which lasted from 1914 to 1918, had considerable personal bearing on him. For one thing, he was cut off from his regular European tours. Moreover, his longtime assistant Franz Kukol, a former military officer, was called back to Austria for the duration of the war.

During the war years Harry concentrated on refining his act by touring America extensively. He also tried moving away from his emphasis on escapes and challenges, by returning to his first love—straight magic. After the war was over, Houdini also began experimenting with a new medium, motion pictures, in an attempt to reach an even larger audience.

## All Magic

For some time, Harry had been interested in moving the emphasis of his show back to his first professional acts, of magic and illusion. He wanted to de-emphasize the strenuous escapes that had long been his hallmark. No doubt, the reason lay largely in the physical demands of the escapes: Houdini was more than forty years old, and although he was still in excellent

shape, his body was no longer as quick, sturdy, and resilient as it had been.

In the spring of 1914, Houdini debuted his new all-magic evening. Bess was back on stage for the first time in years, to

*Houdini and Bess returned to the stage together when Houdini shifted his emphasis away from escapes back to magic and illusions.*

*Houdini performed one of his most spectacular illusions, the vanishing elephant trick, before astonished audiences at New York's Hippodrome Stadium.*

help Houdini perform the trunk substitution act from the old days. Little in the show, in fact, was completely new; it consisted mainly of illusions that Houdini revived from earlier shows, either his own or those of other great magicians.

One typical highlight was the "Expanding Cube," a stunning illusion that had been invented by the German magician Buatier De Kolta and later purchased by Houdini. In this trick, Houdini displayed a small cube, eight inches on a side. When he fired a pistol or shouted a command, the cube instantly expanded to have three-foot sides, and when it was lifted up a beautiful female assistant was revealed.

Another of Houdini's most famous illusions, if only for the sheer scale of the effect, was the vanishing elephant. He introduced this stunt at New York's Hippo-

drome Stadium in 1918, using a 10,000-pound elephant named Jennie.

Houdini performed this trick on several occasions and then stopped. He gave as his reason the strict wartime rationing then in effect. "I made two disappear a day," he later wrote. "That is twelve a week. Mr. [Herbert] Hoover said that I was exhausting the elephant supply of the world."[47]

## Upside Down and Trussed

Also during this time, Houdini began performing a spectacular new promotional stunt that relied not on elaborate illusion but on strength and stamina. It would eventually become one of his best-known and most requested acts. The stunt in-

## An Elephant Disappears

*As quoted in Milbourne Christopher's* Houdini: The Untold Story, *the entertainment newspaper* Variety *made the following comments about the vanishing elephant trick.*

"Houdini puts his title of premiere escape artist behind him and becomes the Master Magician. The elephant was led on the stage by its trainer with Houdini watchfully standing by for another escape if the Asiatic product declared war. Nothing happened excepting Houdini made the elephant do a little magic by making a piece of sugar disappear, Houdini supplying but one piece through the high cost of sugar by the lump. In the immediate vicinity was a 'cabinet' that would not fit an ordinary stage, but would Houdini's four-legged subject.

The attendants turned the cabinet around. It only required fifteen of them to do it. Nothing there, open back and front. One would swear he was looking at the back drop [curtain that separated the rear of the stage from the backstage area] directly through the cabinet. The trainer marched the mammoth in a circle around his lodging house and then led the brute into it. Curtains closed. Curtains opened. No elephant. No trap. No papier maché animal [no dummy elephant]. It had gone. . . . Mr. Houdini has provided a headache [of a mystery] for every child in New York. . . . The matinee crowds will worry themselves into sleep nightly wondering what Houdini did with his elephant."

volved escaping from a straitjacket while hanging upside down from the top cornice, or ledge, of a tall building. Naturally, this spectacle drew huge crowds and gridlocked traffic for blocks around—exactly the sort of public uproar Houdini wanted.

The actual escape from the jacket could be accomplished quickly, but Houdini usually played it out for fifteen or twenty minutes to maximize the suspense. He later remarked that escaping from the jacket while hanging upside down was ac-

tually easier than doing it upright, although it naturally seemed much more difficult to onlookers.

Early on Houdini learned how dangerous these performances could be when a high wind slammed him into the side of a building and he was badly bruised. After that, Houdini always made sure he had a safety line attached to his ankles. Although he never had to use it, he made sure the other end of the safety line was held by an assistant at a window of the building, so that he could be pulled inside quickly in case of an accident.

On one occasion, in San Francisco, Houdini performed his upside-down straitjacket act from a downtown building to publicize his current appearances in the city. As it happened, Houdini's brother Theo Hardeen was also performing at a rival theater.

As Harry hung upside down in his straitjacket, Theo played a dirty trick on him: he had men move through the huge crowd below, passing out cards with his picture and the words, "Hardeen, Appearing All This Week at the Pantages."

Theo expected his brother to give him a hard time about the prank, but he heard nothing at all. Soon afterward, though, Houdini got his revenge. He invited Theo and his wife, along with several other guests, to a lavish dinner at his hotel.

Nothing unusual happened until the meal was over. Houdini announced that it was time for him to leave for his performance at the theater. He stood up, shook hands with his guests all around, and left—but not before handing his brother the check.

## Notes on Escapes

Like most magicians and escape artists, Houdini had a wide range of stock acts that he could perform to vary a steady diet of his more sensational performances. These less famous routines ranged from

*Houdini tests the ropes from which he will later dangle headfirst and escape from a straitjacket (left). After releasing himself from the jacket, Houdini holds his arms out wide for his audience to see.*

"second-sight" mindreading to escapes from "ordinary" restraints, such as giant paper bags and large canvas mailbags.

Houdini was constantly inspired by his surroundings to try new things. Once he saw a windmill in Holland and arranged to be roped to it. But he also borrowed liberally from the tried-and-true ideas of other magicians. As Walter B. Gibson, an editor of Houdini's books on magic, notes

> Houdini was not radical in his work: it is evident from his notes that he relied on accepted methods, but increased their effectiveness by improving or disguising them.[48]

Throughout his career, Houdini kept notes about possible new escapes and tricks as the ideas occurred to him. Sometimes these thoughts were written on whatever was handy, such as hotel or steamship stationery. Most often, however, they were written and illustrated in loose-leaf notebooks.

## Benefits and Free Shows

Houdini tried to enlist in the army in 1917, when America entered the war. He was informed that, at age forty-three, he

### The Secret of His Success

*According to Harold Kellock in* Houdini: His Life Story, *Houdini once made these comments about the secret of his success.*

"My chief task has been to conquer fear. When I am stripped and manacled, nailed securely within a weighted packing case and thrown into the sea, or when I am buried alive under six feet of earth, it is necessary to preserve absolute serenity of spirit. I have to work with great delicacy and lightning speed. If I grow panicky I am lost. And if something goes wrong, if there is some little accident or mishap, some slight miscalculation, I am lost unless all my faculties are working on high, free from mental tension or strain. The public sees only the thrill of the accomplished trick; they have no conception of the tortuous preliminary self-training that was necessary to conquer fear.

My second secret has been, by equally vigorous self-training, to enable me to do remarkable things with my body, to make not one muscle or a group of muscles, but *every* muscle, a responsive worker, quick and sure for its part, to make my fingers super-fingers in dexterity, and to train my toes to do the work of fingers."

was too old. One newspaper, the New York *Clipper*, queried editorially, "Could Houdini, who gets out of everything, escape from military service?"[49] Unable to serve in combat, he instead spent considerable time during the war years performing free for soldiers and organizing shows to raise money for Liberty Bonds, the proceeds of which aided the war effort.

Even Houdini's regular stage shows during this period incorporated patriotic elements. In one trick he put a sheet of glass on a small table, then placed a transparent fish bowl on top of that. To the water in the bowl he added red and blue liquids, mixing them together. The fishbowl's top was then sealed with a paper drumhead.

Houdini bared his right hand to the elbow, broke through the paper, and pulled out four hundred feet of silk streamers. Next, he drew out a succession of giant flags that stretched from one end of the stage to the other. In the middle of these was the Stars and Stripes. As a finale, Houdini reached into the American flag and pulled out a live eagle.

At the shows he performed for "doughboys," as American soldiers were called, Houdini would delight his audiences by producing five-dollar gold coins from the air and throwing them into the audience as souvenirs. He claimed later that he had distributed $7,000 to soldiers in this way.

Also during the war, Houdini invented a new piece of equipment for the navy—the result of a failed escape attempt. He had long dreamed of escaping from within a solid block of ice. He experimented with climbing into a large tank wearing a diving helmet and suit that held enough air for a ten-minute submersion, then having a fast-freezing liquid solution poured in. But he caught a severe cold while testing the device, and the freezing solution could not be perfected. The plan was abandoned.

However, as a result of his experiments, Houdini developed an improved quick-release device for diving suits. He donated his idea to the navy and wrote to a friend, "So my work as an entertainer has served as something better after all, that is, if there is really anything better than making people forget their worries."[50] To his disappointment, however, the navy never used his idea.

## The Pack Rat

In the rare moments when he wasn't on the road, Houdini spent time in New York, at his home on West 113th Street, organizing his ever-increasing library and his many other collections. Houdini loved books; even on tour, he insisted on bringing hundreds of pounds of them along. He distrusted both warehouse storage and the red tape involved with shipping items from overseas, so new additions to the collections acquired while on the road simply joined the traveling library.

Houdini even hired a full-time librarian, an elderly Englishman named Alfred Becks, to take care of his book collection. Becks was also a collector, though he had less money than his employer. Becks once made the mistake of telling Houdini about an especially rare set of books on the theater that he hoped to buy for himself at auction. On the day of the sale, however, the representative of another collector outbid him. Becks was extremely

*An avid collector and book lover, Houdini insisted on bringing his hundreds of pounds of books on tour with him.*

## Saturday Matinees

Houdini was a man of intense but short-lived passions, such as his brief, all-consuming interest in flying. Toward the end of the war, his restless interests turned in a new direction: the movies. Although he had not been impressed by the medium when he saw his first film in Paris, he now believed that movies offered a logical way of reaching vast audiences, as well as of creating illusions that would be impossible to present onstage.

His first venture was a silent film (as all movies were then), a serial called *The Master Mystery*. Serials were common in the

*A movie poster advertises* The Master Mystery.

disappointed, but he never found out that the successful bidder had been working for Houdini, who wanted the theater books for his own collection. Houdini hid the books in his basement and didn't add them to his library until after Becks died.

Besides books, Houdini's main interest in collecting lay in unusual locks, handcuffs, magic memorabilia, and autographs, including those of men who had signed the Declaration of Independence. But he also accumulated much more than that, including a Bible signed by Martin Luther, Edgar Allan Poe's portable writing desk, and the first electric chair used at the Auburn, New York, prison. The chair had been on exhibit at a dime museum Houdini performed in during his early days.

early days of motion pictures; one "chapter" in a story would be shown each week, with each exciting installment ending in a way that ensured a return audience.

*The Master Mystery* played for 13 successive Saturday matinees across the country in 1919. The story line concerned a company, International Patents, Inc., which was controlled by a ruthless tyrant in a castle fortress. Below the castle was a secret storeroom called the Graveyard of Genius, where models of inventions were kept; these had been purchased from inventors to keep progress from interfering with the company's own interests.

Houdini played Quentin Locke, a secret agent of the Department of Justice. Each week, a robot called the Automaton, controlled by the evil genius, used a different method to try and kill Locke: binding him in barbed wire and letting acid spill toward him, tying him underneath a freight elevator, or drugging him with the fumes from poisoned candles. In the final episode, Locke prevailed by inventing an explosive gas bullet that penetrated the steel body of the robot to reveal a human inside.

## The First Feature Film

*The Master Mystery* was successful enough that Houdini moved on to make feature films for Hollywood. Naturally, they all included a number of daring escapes.

Houdini choreographed these escapes and usually did his own stunts. One of the most spectacular stunts, however, was unplanned, and—despite the stories Houdini told afterward—was not performed by Houdini himself.

The Master Mystery *was so successful that it was translated into other languages and distributed internationally.*

It happened during the filming of his first feature, *The Grim Game*. Here is Houdini's version:

> I was 3,000 feet up in an airplane circling above another machine. The plan was for me to drop from my plane into the cockpit of the other by means of a rope. I was dangling from the rope end ready for the leap.
>
> Suddenly, the two planes crashed together, the propellers locked, and we started plunging downward towards the earth—and Eternity. I was helpless—but strangely unafraid. A lifetime passed in an instant. The crash will come. I shall be gone. But it is not all. There is another life. There

## Exposing Secrets

*Walter B. Gibson, one of the editors of* Houdini on Magic, *comments on why Houdini sometimes revealed secrets.*

"To some readers it will come as a surprise to learn that Houdini exposed some handcuff secrets, considering that his career depended on them. It might also be assumed that he reserved such writings until he was through with the secrets concerned. Quite to the contrary, these represent some of his earliest literary efforts, published while he was still actively engaged in baffling the public with the very artifices he discloses.

Houdini's purpose was twofold: He wanted to establish himself as the pioneer of the Challenge Act and at the same time worry his imitators by giving away the more common devices upon which they depended. Frequently, along with crediting himself with certain inventions, Houdini disclaimed inferior methods as though he would never have stooped to their use. So even Houdini's exposures carry the implication that his own work approached the supernormal.

However, . . . when Houdini reserved methods for his own use, it was not necessarily because they were superior, but because they were less known than those which he did explain. About the only thing conclusively proved was that the exposure of such mysteries only increased public interest. . . ."

---

must be! was the comforting thought in my head. But fate ruled otherwise.

By a miracle we righted into a half glide, and though they [the airplanes] were smashed into splinters by their terrific impact with the ground, I was miraculously unhurt.[51]

The real story is a little different. The script called for a midair transfer, all right, and there really was an unplanned crash. However, Houdini was safely on the ground at the time. Irvin Willat, the film's director, recalls that he was strongly opposed to having his valuable star perform such a dangerous maneuver: "Houdini thought he was going to do it [the stunt], but he was a very intelligent man and gave me no argument when I told him he wasn't.[52]

The stuntman who actually performed the midair transfer was a young pilot who had flown in the war. No one was seriously hurt when the planes crashed. The collision was caught on film, and the script was hastily rewritten to incorporate the spectacular footage.

## Box-Office Bombs

Houdini made a second Hollywood film, *Terror Island*. Neither it nor *The Grim Game* was a huge success, however. Most critics blamed Houdini's wooden acting for his lack of box-office appeal, but Houdini was convinced that bad distribution and management were the real problems. In 1921, certain that he could make a more successful movie on his own, Houdini formed a production company that made two more films, *The Man from Beyond* and *Haldane of the Secret Service*.

Houdini could control everything now. He wrote the scripts, chose the locations, starred, directed, edited—even handled all the publicity. He formed a film development company and put his brother Theo in charge of it. There is some evidence that he was helped with his scripts by the famous horror writer H.P. Lovecraft, although Houdini always took full credit.

According to Houdini, the script for *The Man from Beyond* was written in ten days. It concerns a man who had been frozen in a block of ice for a century; when an Arctic expedition found and freed him, he began a search for his lost love. She was long since dead, of course, but she had a great-granddaughter who happened to be her exact double. In the

*Two scenes from* The Grim Game *reveal some of the stunts that Houdini choreographed himself. The stunts were not enough to carry the film, however, and it did not fare well commercially.*

*Scenes from* The Man from Beyond *(below) and* Haldane of the Secret Service *(right). Neither film was a box office success. While Houdini blamed bad distribution and management, critics blamed Houdini's stiff acting style.*

movie's big finale, shot at Niagara Falls, Houdini saved the heroine from the brink of the waterfall after her canoe had already gone over. Houdini did this stunt himself, equipped with a safety rope.

*Haldane of the Secret Service* also had an action-packed plot. Houdini played a government agent who was pitted against a gang of counterfeiters. They led him from New York to London, to Paris, and finally to a monastery in the French countryside. There, they strapped him to a giant waterwheel and left him to die—but, of course, he escaped and triumphed.

Although Houdini publicized these movies relentlessly, often showing them on the same bill with his personal appearances, he never achieved huge successes at the box office. For some reason, the

*Houdini in a movie scene with actress Mito Naldi. Houdini's charisma did not translate to the screen, especially when it came to romantic scenes.*

charisma he displayed onstage did not translate to the screen.

One reason, certainly, was his stiff acting; he was terrific with daredevil stunts, but wooden when doing everything else. He was so embarrassed to kiss his leading ladies on screen that he would keep glancing at Bess, who was off-camera. He felt so guilty at embracing another woman that he even gave Bess $5 for each screen kiss he was forced to perform. At a time when daring on-screen lovers like Rudolph Valentino were the rage, such shyness did not draw audiences.

Houdini finally was forced to admit defeat at the box office. As Milbourne Christopher has written:

> He [Houdini] read the reviews with dismay. He compared his cost sheets with the income statements. Sadly, he removed his pending productions from the active file and brought his career as a picture producer to an abrupt finish.[53]

As quickly as he had abandoned his other passions, Houdini left moviemaking behind.

# 6 Exposing Spiritualism

After the war, Houdini found himself at another crossroad. He no longer needed to perform benefit shows. His career as a film producer was over. He was able once again to tour the lucrative European circuit; but he found that vaudeville had changed.

After the long years of the war, audiences weren't looking for thrills and excitement. They instead demanded light comedy, romance, sentiment, and song. Houdini's daring escapes and powerful illusions were no longer guaranteed crowd pleasers.

He started experiencing the ultimate insult for a performer: to be dropped from star billing. This served to fire up his competitive energies even more; as biographer William Lindsay Gresham put it, "Houdini knew that the specter of oblivion was haunting him more closely than ever before in his life."[54] He had to work harder than ever at drawing audiences in.

Late in 1919, Houdini sailed for England for the first time since the war. His act was a sort of "greatest hits"—a compendium of his most famous magic tricks and escapes. But it was also the beginning of a new element that he incorporated into both his personal life and his public shows: spiritualism. Spiritualism—or, more accurately, the attempt to debunk

it—would become one of the most important parts of Houdini's life in his later years.

*When Houdini no longer headlined performances, he took up another interest: exposing psychic frauds.*

*Houdini demonstrates the tricks used by phony spiritualists. As part of his crusade to debunk spiritualism, he offered $10,000 to anyone who could create a psychic phenomenon that he could not disprove.*

## Houdini and Spiritualism

Spiritualism is a general term for faith in various supernatural or psychic phenomena, such as extrasensory perception or experiencing the dead speaking to us. Spiritualism has fascinated the human race for thousands of years, and the debate about the validity of the claims that have been made for it is very much with us today.

Houdini had an intense love/hate relationship with spiritualism all his life. He passionately wanted to believe the claims that were made by the spiritualists. Especially after the death of his mother, he wanted to be able to communicate with the dead. But he knew too much about fooling the public to be taken in by any of the mediums he saw.

There is evidence that Houdini's interest in spiritualism stemmed from the earliest days of his career, but it intensified greatly as he grew older. In fact, his cru-sade to expose phony "spirit mediums" dominated his career in the years after the war. (Today, a more common term for "spirit medium" is "channeler.") These efforts included a standing offer of $10,000, which was never claimed, to anyone who could create a psychic phenomenon that he couldn't reproduce by nonsupernatural means. His stage shows also included lengthy demonstrations of the tricks that phony mediums used.

Nothing in Houdini's career created more controversy than his attacks on phony psychics. Walter B. Gibson, who edited Houdini's notebooks, writes:

It is difficult today to picture the stir that Houdini's activities fomented [stirred up]. The wave of spiritualism that followed World War I had been fanned to the proportions of a tempest. . . . In taking the opposite side of the question, Houdini automatically plunged himself into something more than a controversy; namely, a full-fledged career.[55]

## Bess on Houdini's Superstitions

*Bess, quoted in Harold Kellock's* Houdini: His Life Story, *reflects on the irony of Houdini's own strongly held superstitions, which he believed in wholeheartedly even as he sought to debunk spiritual beliefs.*

"[Early in our marriage] he gradually drove away my [own] superstitions. Among other things he taught me the secret of mindreading and all the arts of legerdemain [sleight of hand], including how to go into trances and tell fortunes. My inside view of the mechanism of such phenomena did more than anything else to exorcise the ghosts and hobgoblins that had peopled my world.

In due time I learned that while Houdini had attacked my superstitions relentlessly, he duly preserved certain little taboos of his own. For instance, he, who was ordinarily without fear, and deliberately risked his life in dangerous public exhibitions week after week for many years, would take no risks whatever on Friday the thirteenth. On that day he would cut out all hazardous acts from his stage show and would perform no outdoor feats. On one occasion he had been advertised to release himself from handcuffs and straight-jacket [sic] while suspended head downward from a very tall building on a Friday the thirteenth. There was always danger of a mischance and a fatal fall, in such dizzy exhibitions, and Houdini's assistants realised that if Houdini gave a thought to the date he would simply quit. Accordingly they fixed up a false calendar, and displayed it prominently in his dressing-room, so that for Houdini that day was the fourteenth and he played his dangerous part successfully. Fortunately he seldom noticed dates, so it was easy to fool him."

## Half-Believing

Throughout his career, Houdini visited thousands of psychics and saw countless displays of apparently impossible marvels. In every case, however, Houdini was able to figure out how these seemingly miraculous deeds were performed.

Nonetheless, his willingness to believe kept him searching out new mediums in the hope of finding the genuine article. The shabby tricks he uncovered disappointed him, but they also fueled his determination to persevere. In a 1922 newspaper article, he wrote:

> My mind is open. I am perfectly willing to believe but . . . I have never seen or heard anything that could convince one there is a possibility of communication with the loved ones who have gone beyond.[56]

Houdini continued to expose frauds who passed themselves off as genuine psychics, even while he himself still half-believed. He had many personal idiosyncrasies that showed his willingness to believe in spiritualism. For instance, he

*An advertisement announces an appearance by the great Houdini in a show that includes magic, illusions, and spiritual exposés.*

was highly superstitious and would never knowingly perform dangerous stunts on a Friday the Thirteenth.

He also formed solemn pacts with his wife, his personal secretary, and other close friends and associates. The first to die, it was agreed, was to try and reach the others from beyond the grave. Each had a code word with which to identify himself to the survivors.

At the same time, Houdini wrote extensively on the subject of spiritualistic fraud, and his book entitled *A Magician Among the Spirits* was a best-seller. Here Houdini provided evidence that the founders of modern spiritualism had deliberately deceived the public. Milbourne Christopher writes that this book was "loaded with awkward facts that most true believers either had not known about or preferred to forget."[57] Houdini then added insult to injury by charging for lectures explaining how the public had been tricked.

## Public Debunking

Spiritualism was an interesting but not obsessive topic for Houdini until the death of his mother. In the years after 1913, however, Houdini became engrossed in it. He devoted large portions of his performances to demonstrations of psychic fraud. He lectured extensively on the subject, neglecting better-paying engagements. And he donated considerable time to unmasking phonies in whatever town he happened to be in.

The public speeches, in the form of either lectures or theatrical performances, emphasized his opinion that for many people, spiritualism was a legitimate religion. He stated strongly his belief that all people should be allowed to worship as they saw fit, as long as they stayed within the law and harmed no one.

But he also pointed out that he had yet to experience a genuinely unexplainable psychic phenomenon. His main desire was to keep frauds and con artists from fooling the public. As Milbourne Christopher writes:

> Houdini . . . was genuinely disturbed by spiritualism's growing hold on the gullible, eager-to-believe American public. . . . His years as an entertainer and a student of deception had prepared him to be a public benefactor, an effective crusader against the cheats and charlatans who fleeced the bereaved.[58]

Houdini adjusted his theatrical performances to include demonstrations of typical psychic tricks. For instance, he would seat himself on stage, with his hands and feet held down by the hands and feet of volunteers. The volunteers wore hoods to reproduce the lack of visibility in a darkened room.

"Psychic" bumping noises would then be heard, which were actually produced by Houdini banging his head on a table without letting his hooded guests know he had moved. Bells and tambourines would also be sounded; these were set off by Houdini's foot. His feet were supposedly being held securely down by the feet of volunteers, making movement impossible. But Houdini would withdraw one foot from a shoe reinforced inside with a special hard shell, ring the bell, and then replace the foot without the volunteers suspecting.

On one tour, he amazed his audiences by predicting which news stories would be the big ones in the paper the next day. People marveled at this talent, until he revealed that he had a direct wire in his dressing room to the city desk of the New York *World*.

Houdini's combination show—part escapes, part magic, part exposés of spiritualism—was a popular and critical success. In the Cincinnati *Commercial Tribune*, one reviewer wrote that the show

> was good fun from start to finish. . . . Houdini manages these magical shows just a bit better than anyone else. . . . There's one big difference between Houdini on a vaudeville bill and Houdini in his own show. In the latter instance there's more of him. Ergo, the show is better.[59]

## Reformed and Unreformed Mediums

For a time, Houdini hired a private investigator to travel with him, and in each city she compiled information about local mediums by posing as a curious believer. Sometimes Houdini's niece, Julia Sawyer, accompanied the private eye. Onstage, Houdini would ask the mediums to come forward and challenge him for the $10,000. Many tried, but none ever succeeded.

One medium in Syracuse, New York, produced a spirit message for Julia from a sister she never had, as well as messages from her supposedly dead mother and brother (who in fact were both alive). After the séance, as such attempts to com-

## Houdini on Spiritualist Frauds

*In 1923 Houdini expressed his attitude toward spiritualism in a newspaper piece, reprinted in* Houdini on Magic, *edited by Walter B. Gibson.*

"When I started to investigate Spiritualism more than twenty-five years ago, I did so with an open mind and a sincere desire to learn if truth was involved in Spiritualism. During all those years, more than a quarter of a century, and up to the present moment, I have not received any convincing evidence, and of all the mediums I have encountered, not one of them has satisfied me with the genuineness of psychical phenomena. To the contrary, I have never failed to detect a fraud, or at least a possible solution on a perfectly rational basis. . . .

It has been stated in print by a staunch believer in spiritualism [Sir Arthur Conan Doyle] that I possess psychic power, but were I to accept that statement as being true, I should be pluming myself with false feathers.

The belief in Spiritualism is getting to be a very serious thing, and it is high time that the truth should be established beyond peradventure of doubt by undeniable evidence. . . .

I am not an irretrievable sceptic. I am not hopelessly prejudiced. I am perfectly willing to believe, and my mind is wide open; but I have, as yet, to be convinced. I am perfectly willing, but the evidence must be sane and conclusive."

municate with the dead were called, Julia and the detective invited the medium to come and visit Julia's aged uncle, a gray-haired man slumped in a wheelchair and attended by a nurse.

The psychic produced a message for the old man that was as false as the earlier ones. At that, the old man suddenly took off his whiskers to reveal himself as Houdini. The nurse was also a ringer: in fact, he was a newspaper reporter. The medium then admitted his trickery, but justified it by saying that, after all, he and Houdini were in the same business. "Not so!" Houdini replied indignantly. "I'm a legitimate entertainer, you're a cheat."[60]

One source has speculated that some of Houdini's exposés of mediums, with Houdini dressed in his white wig, were really setups. It is possible that the mediums who were thus exposed knew that their faithful followers would still believe even after Houdini had blasted them; it is also possible that they would be willing to be exposed for a fee. There is no hard evidence that any of the exposés were really setups, but given Houdini's fondness for publicity, it is certainly possible that some "unmaskings" were prearranged.

## Houdini and Conan Doyle

A worthy opponent for Houdini in his crusade against spiritualism was the English writer, Sir Arthur Conan Doyle. Conan Doyle was a physician who became world famous when he created the fictional detective Sherlock Holmes. Sir Arthur and Lady Doyle had long maintained a

*English author Sir Arthur Conan Doyle shakes hands with Houdini. Doyle was convinced that Houdini was a psychic who was unaware of his own powers.*

personal belief in spiritualism. They became firm believers when a psychic friend produced a message from Lady Doyle's brother, who had been killed in the war. The message included intimate details that convinced the author and his wife of its authenticity. Thanks to Conan Doyle's prestige and fame, the writer became a powerful spokesman for the legitimacy of spiritualism.

The two famous men had corresponded for some time before the Doyles and the Houdinis finally met in 1920. Although there was an age difference—Conan Doyle was old enough to be Houdini's father—the couples became friends. Houdini and Conan Doyle also admired each other's intellects and accomplishments.

Despite the age gap, Houdini and Doyle were, in many ways, compatible. They were both men of action, athletes, and passionate crusaders for their beliefs. They were both sentimental romantics, both (even more so than was the custom of the day) chivalrous toward women and devoted to their mothers. Both loved animals and children. Both had been born into poor families but had become rich and famous through personal initiative.

But they differed strongly over spiritualism. Sir Arthur was convinced that Houdini was a powerful psychic, who was nevertheless unaware of his remarkable gifts. Houdini, meanwhile, insisted that all his escapes were performed by perfectly explainable, rational means.

Houdini couldn't believe that a man as intelligent as Conan Doyle, a man trained in the rigors of medical science and the creator of the supremely rational Sherlock Holmes, could be so gullible. Conan Doyle found it impossible to understand why Houdini could deny something

## Not a Psychic Force for Evil

*J. Hewat Mackenzie, president of the British College of Psychic Science, firmly believed that Houdini was a psychic who was unaware of his own powers. This passage from his book* Spirit Intercourse *[dealing with spirits], along with Houdini's reply, are quoted in* Houdini's Escapes and Magic, *edited by Walter B. Gibson.*

"Mackenzie: 'The [psychic] force necessary to shoot a bolt within a lock is withdrawn from Houdini, the medium, but it must not be thought that this is the only means by which he can escape from his prison, for at times his body has been dematerialized and withdrawn.'

Houdini: 'I do not claim to free myself from the restraint of fetters and confinements, but positively state that I accomplish my purpose purely by physical, not psychical, means. My methods are perfectly natural, resting on natural laws of physics. I do not *dematerialize* anything: I simply control and manipulate material things in a manner perfectly well understood by myself, and thoroughly accountable for and equally understandable (if not duplicable) by any person to whom I may elect to divulge my secrets. But I hope to carry these secrets to the grave, as they are of no material benefit to mankind, and if they should be used by dishonest persons they might become a serious menace.'"

that seemed obvious—that he, Houdini, himself possessed remarkable supernatural abilities. As Sir Arthur wrote in a letter to Houdini:

Yes, you have driven me to the occult! My reason tells me that you have this wonderful power, for there is no alternative, tho' I have no doubt that, up to a point, your strength and skill avail you.[61]

Time and again, Sir Arthur tried to convince Houdini to believe in his own psychic powers; time and again, Houdini refuted the Englishman's claims. Houdini did not doubt that Conan Doyle's belief was sincere and real, but he remained skeptical. Gradually, their differences forced them apart.

On one occasion, the Doyles invited Houdini to a séance during which Lady Doyle performed automatic writing, which is supposed to come from a disembodied spirit. After entering a trance, Lady Doyle produced a long message, which she insisted was from Houdini's mother. It consisted of vague platitudes along the lines of "Don't worry, my darling, because I am happy."

But Houdini was doubtful, for several reasons. For one thing, the message was in English, a language his mother had never spoken. For another, Lady Doyle had drawn a large cross at the top of the paper, something Houdini's devoutly Jewish mother would never have done. Finally, by coincidence, the séance had been held on Cecilia's birthday—yet that fact was never mentioned in the "message."

On another occasion, Sir Arthur stated in public his belief that a psychic couple called the Zancigs were genuine telepathists, or mind readers. Houdini remembered the Zancigs from their days together on the vaudeville circuit, however, and he knew well the tricks of their mind-reading act. Doyle also sent Houdini to visit a man who produced "spirit photos" of dead people sitting alongside the living, but Houdini proved that the seemingly impossible pictures were double exposures.

Houdini never told the Doyles about his skepticism, out of friendship and respect, but he made some careless statements to the press that offended the Doyles. Gradually, the two men became estranged, and eventually they had a serious falling-out. Their public statements grew more personally vindictive; it was no longer a matter of simple intellectual disagreement.

The final blow came when Houdini wrote to Conan Doyle for some information and got back a short note: "You probably want these extracts in order to twist them in some way against me or my cause."[62] Another letter from Houdini went unanswered, and the correspondence stopped. Houdini bitterly told reporters later that Conan Doyle was a hypocrite and a fake.

Despite it all, Conan Doyle remained convinced of Houdini's psychic abilities. The rabbi who presided at Houdini's funeral had stated then that the magician possessed a supernatural power. Conan Doyle was confident that this remark, coming from a prominent religious man on a solemn occassion, validated his own feelings about Houdini's supernatural powers.

## "Margery" and the *Scientific American*

One of the most highly publicized of Houdini's ventures in the area of spiritualism was the case of the mysterious "Margery."

In 1922 Houdini was asked to be on a committee formed by *Scientific American* magazine to investigate psychic phenomena. The committee also included a psychology professor from Harvard and a professor of physics from the Massachusetts Institute of Technology, as well as two men who were sympathetic to spiritualism—a researcher for the American Society for Psychical Research and a well-known writer on psychic phenomena.

The committee met periodically to test anyone who tried to claim the rewards the magazine was offering: $2,000 for a verifiable "spirit photograph" and $2,500 for psychic phenomena produced under strict test conditions. Houdini added his standing $10,000 offer to the *Scientific American* reward money.

At first, there were few applicants. It was easy for a photographer to develop puzzling pictures in his own studio, or for a medium to produce strange phenomena in her own home. Why risk a reputation by being tested by observers familiar with psychology, physics, and the use of trickery?

But in 1923 one psychic couple was bold enough to challenge the committee. A middle-aged Boston surgeon, Dr. Le Roi

Goddard Crandon, had become interested in spiritualism. He further discovered that his wife Mina—a vivacious beauty half his age—had a gift for mediumship. Under her husband's direction, Mina was soon able to move tables around during séances, to make invisible trumpets sound, to produce live pigeons out of thin air, and to stop clocks in distant rooms by sheer "mental concentration."

When she began claiming that she could also channel her dead brother Walter, her fame as a medium grew. "Walter's" vocabulary was very salty—definitely not that of a proper Boston society woman. That detail alone convinced many people of Mina's authenticity; they simply couldn't believe that a lady was capable of swearing.

Houdini was unavailable for the first tests of the *Scientific American* committee, and the group's secretary, J. Malcolm Bird, wrote two enthusiastic articles about Mrs. Crandon for the magazine, disguising her identity by using the name "Margery." When Houdini found out that the committee had met without him, he was furious and demanded his own audience.

Houdini was able to expose Margery as a fraud in a single session, during which the medium caused a luminous board to move and a bell to ring, although her hands and feet were apparently held immobile by committee members. She didn't know that earlier in the day, Houdini had worn a tight bandage on his right leg beneath the knee.

Houdini rolled up his trouser leg during the séance so that Margery could put her foot against his leg, to prove that she was not moving any part of her body. Houdini's skin was so tender that any small

*As a member of the committee formed by* Scientific American *to expose spiritualism, Houdini examines a prop that was used during a fake séance.*

motion was immediately felt. Houdini felt her leg sliding as she inched her foot over to tip the luminous board and press her toe on the bell box.

But the committee was not convinced, and wanted another session with the Crandons. For this, Houdini built a "fraud-preventer" box that completely enclosed Margery while she was seated. Only her head and hands, which extended through holes in the box, were outside. Houdini also insisted that someone other than her husband hold her hands during the session. When she was locked into the box, and without Dr. Crandon holding her hands, there were no supernatural phenomena.

## Government Testimony

Houdini's crusade against fraudulent mediums went as far as a speech to the U.S. House of Representatives. During a theatrical run in Philadelphia, he traveled to Washington, D.C., to testify before a congressional committee that was reviewing a bill to ban fortune-telling in the District of Columbia. Houdini spoke in its favor. He emphasized his respect for genuine believers in spiritualism or any other religion, but said:

> There are only two kinds of mediums, those who are mental degenerates and who ought to be under observation, and those who are deliberate cheats and frauds. . . . In thirty-five years I have never seen one genuine medium.[63]

Mediums and their supporters filled the hall where the committee was meeting. During the hearing, Houdini challenged them with a question he often used to stump so-called psychics while on tour: "Can you state the name by which my mother called me when I was little?" According to a reporter for the New York *Morning Telegraph*, a palm reader who was standing just outside the committee-room door said, "She probably called him an incipient damn fool."[64]

## On a Ship with Teddy Roosevelt

Besides his congressional testimony, Houdini was able on another occasion to expose fraudulent spiritualism to a politician. While sailing back to America from an en-gagement in Europe, Harry happened to be on the same ship as former president Theodore Roosevelt, who was also famous as a world explorer. The magician was persuaded to put on a special show for Roosevelt and the rest of the passengers.

Houdini asked Roosevelt to write a question "for the spirits to answer." Roosevelt borrowed a book lying nearby to use as a desk, turning his back so that Houdini couldn't see what he wrote. Houdini asked him to put the paper between a pair of "magic" slates; when the slates were reopened, inside was a map in colored chalk. On the map, a route was clearly marked and an arrow pointed to a particular spot.

An amazed Roosevelt announced that the map showed a section of South America into which he had led an expedition the preceding winter. He then revealed

*While traveling on the same ship as Theodore Roosevelt, Houdini took the opportunity to perform for the former president.*

## Congressional Testimony

*In* Houdini: The Untold Story, *Milbourne Christopher quotes from Houdini's testimony before the congressional committee that was deliberating a law to ban fortune-telling in the District of Columbia.*

"Please understand that, emphatically, I am not attacking a religion. I respect every genuine believer in spiritualism or any other religion. . . . But this thing they call spiritualism, wherein a medium intercommunicates with the dead, is a fraud from start to finish. There are only two kinds of mediums, those who are mental degenerates and who ought to be under observation, and those who are deliberate cheats and frauds. I would not believe a fraudulent medium under oath; perjury means nothing to them.

How can you call it a religion when you get men and women in a room together and they feel each other's hands and bodies? The inspirational mediums are not quite as bad as that. But they guess, and by 'fishing' methods and by reading the obituary notices get the neurotics to believe that they hear voices and see forms. In thirty-five years I have never seen one genuine medium."

*Houdini presents a congressional committee with evidence against fraudulent fortune-tellers.*

his question: "Where did I spend Christmas?" The question had been accurately answered.

Houdini then showed how he had performed this amazing trick. During his preliminary patter, he had craftily planted the idea of what question to ask in Roosevelt's mind. In addition, he had made sure that there was a sheet of carbon paper under the dust jacket of the book that "just happened" to be lying near Roosevelt, in handy reach for use as a desk.

Finally, Houdini drew on some inside knowledge: he was aware that the South American journey was on Roosevelt's mind, because the explorer had just written a series of articles about it for the London *Telegraph*. In fact, while in London, Houdini had learned that one of these articles, "Celebrating Christmas at a Camp in the Andes," was due to be published soon. Houdini had thus created the illusion of psychic powers through a combination of preparation, clever psychology, and luck.

## Rahman Bey

One of the last spiritualists Houdini exposed was an "Italo-Arab mystic" (as he called himself) who went by the name of Rahman Bey. Bey claimed that he could remain submerged in water for nearly half an hour in a zinc-lined coffin that had been soldered shut. It was his mystic Eastern powers, Bey claimed, that enabled him to enter a cataleptic (suspended) state, because the coffin held only enough air for three minutes of breathing.

After Houdini had been critical of Rahman Bey on several occasions, the mystic's press agent challenged Houdini to duplicate his client's feat. Houdini accepted the dare and had his employees build a coffin the exact size of Bey's. He then conducted a public performance in a swimming pool to show that contrary to Bey's allegations, the coffin could store far more than three minutes' worth of air.

Before he descended into the pool, Houdini said to reporters in his typically melodramatic way:

> If I die, it will be the will of God and my own foolishness. I am going to prove that the copybook maxims are wrong when they say a man can live but three minutes without air, and I am not going to pretend to be in a cataleptic state either.[65]

In fact, Houdini lasted an hour and a half. He did it, first of all, by eating proteins and carbohydrates for twenty-four hours before the stunt, to halve his need for oxygen intake. He took several deep breaths before the cover was fastened, and he made a minimum amount of movement once the coffin was sealed. He stayed relaxed, breathing rhythmically and shallowly. He knew that the worst thing would be to panic, which would cause him to breathe deeply and use up the air quickly.

Houdini's pulse rate was 142 when he came out of the coffin; it had been 84 when he had been lowered into the water. The only ill effects of the ordeal were slight feelings of dizziness and tiredness. In a letter to a magician friend, he later wrote:

> There is a rumor going around that there is a gimmick to [the coffin]. I pledge my word of honor there isn't a thing to it excepting to lie down and keep quiet.
>
> I trained for three weeks in water to get my lungs accustomed to battle without air, and after one hour, [I] did have to struggle and believe only due to the training was I able to stay so long. Rest assured there is no gimmick, no trick at all—simply lying on your back and breathing shallow breaths is all you do. Did it twice in a coffin with a glass top to test myself. There is no doubt in my mind that anyone can do it.[66]

*Houdini climbs into a coffin before performing an underwater stunt (left).*
*Assistants lower the airtight coffin into the water (right). Before the coffin was*
*sealed and submerged underwater, Houdini remarked, "If I die, it will be the*
*will of God and my own foolishness."*

Many years later, in 1958, a magician called the Amazing Randi duplicated the feat for British television. The coffin he used was the same size as Houdini's, but Randi was younger and smaller. He stayed down for just over two hours.

After he was through exposing Rahman Bey, Houdini had an elaborate bronze casket made for the then-extravagant sum of $2,500. He planned to use it to duplicate his exposé of Rahman Bey on his next tour, which began in the fall of 1926. The escape, in Houdini's mind, took the place of the "Buried Alive" stunt he had been forced to abandon many years before. As fate would have it, however, this was to be Houdini's last tour—and the casket was very nearly his final resting place.

# 7 Houdini's Last Days

In the summer of 1926, the Houdinis rented a vacation cottage at Glen Head, New York, which is on Long Island. After only a few days of swimming and sunning himself, however, Harry grew impatient with being inactive.

He began thinking up ideas for the new show he planned to take on the road. It would be an entire evening that combined the best he had to offer: magic involving disappearing lamps and female assistants who turned into rosebushes, such escapes as the Chinese water torture and coffin stunts, and a "spook show" (as he called it) featuring an antipsychic lecture and demonstrations.

The Chinese water torture cell had become Houdini's most famous and requested act. Houdini's hands would be shackled and his feet enclosed in a sturdy mahogany stock. Houdini would then be suspended upside down from ropes attached to the wooden stock, lifted high, and lowered into a huge glass tank filled with water. The top would be securely fastened, and Houdini's assistants would

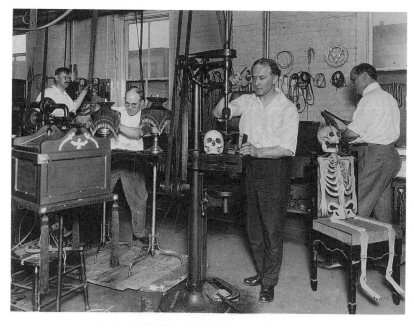

*In his workshop, Houdini prepares props to use in his upcoming magic shows.*

stand dramatically by with fire axes, ready to break the glass if Houdini failed to escape. He never did.

Houdini took his new show on the road in the fall of 1926—a two-and-a-half-hour extravaganza, with the star on stage nearly every minute. Houdini put all his energy into his shows—to the exclusion of any other consideration. Such intensity of focus would prove to be his undoing.

## Bess Falls Ill

In many ways, Houdini relied for his very existence on his wife. The couple never had children, and except for Theo, Harry was not especially close to his brothers and sister. Thus after his mother died, Bess became his closest companion and, in many ways, his keeper.

Once, when he was going on tour without her, she packed a week's worth of shirts for him to wear. She marked each one with a label indicating the day on which it was to be worn. When the magician got home, all but one of the shirts lay untouched, still in the order of packing. Bess also washed Harry's ears every day, because he'd never learned to do it properly himself. She often said he was "the most helpless man in the world."[67]

Houdini was also in the habit of writing Bess a love letter every day. A typical note that Bess found when she woke up read as follows: "Adorable Sun Shine of my life. I have had my coffee, have washed out this glass and am on my way to business. Houdini. My darling I love you." Even after they had argued, Houdini would leave her similar notes: "Honey lamb, sweetheart. It is 8 A.M. No one pays

*Houdini always credited his wife Bess for his many successes.*

any attention to me. So even though you do get a 'tantrum' and give me hell, I'd rather have you with me."[68]

Houdini always insisted that Bess was the sole reason for his success. He depended on her almost entirely to run his life for him. So it is natural that he became frantic when, one morning in mid-October, she awoke nauseated and feverish in their hotel suite in Providence, Rhode Island.

When he himself was injured, Houdini never saw a doctor unless Bess cried, pleaded, and threatened to leave him. When she fell ill, however, a doctor was by her bedside in minutes. A diagnosis of ptomaine poisoning, a kind of food poisoning, was made, and rest and constant care were the doctor's orders.

Houdini hired a nurse and stayed up with Bess all night. He did not sleep at all the next day except for a nap between his matinee and evening shows at the Providence Opera House. Bess and the rest of the troupe then went on to the next stop on the tour, Albany, New York. Houdini, though, had to return briefly to New York City to consult with his lawyer.

## The Show Goes On

Houdini caught a train to Albany as quickly as possible when he finished his New York business, but he never slept well on trains and arrived in the state capital exhausted. Bess was still weak and in bed.

Despite having gone three nights without sleep, Houdini went on with his evening show. During the performance, while he was being lifted up upside down in the Chinese water torture escape, the frame that held his legs in place jerked suddenly and he injured his foot.

His assistants helped him down, but he found he couldn't stand. A doctor in the audience examined the injury and informed Houdini that his ankle was broken. The doctor advised that the foot be X-rayed and the bone set immediately; Houdini insisted on finishing the show first, however, so the doctor applied an emergency splint. The show went on, but instead of finishing "the upside down," Houdini did his threaded-needle trick, hopping on one foot across the stage as he strung out the thread, and then closed the show with his usual fraud-exposing demonstrations.

Houdini was no stranger to pain, and he refused to remain idle even when severely injured. In Detroit in 1911, he had been fastened into a restraint with such force that the straps used to hold him had burst a blood vessel in one kidney. He bled internally for two weeks before bothering to see a doctor. Houdini was forced to take two weeks off on that occasion, but even then he kept busy with such activities as making notes for books he wanted to write or supervising the unpacking of his treasures at home.

*Against the advice of a doctor, Houdini insisted on finishing a show with an injured foot. Unable to stand on the hurt foot, he performed the threaded-needle trick hopping across the stage on one foot.*

# A Star Attraction

*In* Houdini: The Untold Story, *Milbourne Christopher quotes from the Baltimore* Sun *an account of a typical show during Houdini's last years, featuring his combination of escape, magic, and spiritualism exposé.*

"Mr. Houdini appears and disappears in detachable shirt sleeves at the Academy of Music this week. He is supported by a capable cast of white rabbits, private detectives, pouter pigeons, furniture-movers, and a brown leghorn rooster. The handcuff king fools all of his audience most of the time and most of his audience all of the time. Moreover he has $10,000 in negotiable bonds that [backs up his claim that] he can unscrew the inscrutable [mysterious] when it comes to spiritualism.

Legerdemain lovers lined up for half a block last night when it was time for the curtain. . . . Inside they clapped and whistled just like the folks back home. Up went the curtain. Two of Mr. Houdini's flapper operatives [trendy young female assistants] in colonial disguise drew back a handsome drapery by its tasseled cords. Behind stood Mr. Houdini's mechanical equipment, portable houses and uniformed scene shifters.

Out walked the whole show: Mr. Houdini in person, full dress, and detachable shirt sleeves, which he detached immediately. He hushed the orchestra with a graceful gesture. 'Ladies and gentlemen,' he intoned in traditional fashion. The show was on.

The entertainment, like Mr. Houdini himself, is a vibrant testimonial to the fact that the hand is quicker than the eye. Now you see lamps, flower pots, and ladies of the harem. Now you don't.

He chopped a man to pieces and reassembled him. With feet encased in mahogany stocks, the magician was raised by block and tackle and dumped head first into a steel-lined tank of water and clamped inside like a roast in a pressure cooker. Write your own solution.

A brief lecture and working demonstration on departed spirits concludes a three-act performance. It is in this whirlwind finish that Mr. Houdini displays his roll [of $10,000] and proves spiritualistic bell-ringers as bogus as the Wonderful Wizard of Oz."

Not only was Houdini indifferent to physical pain, he also subscribed to the old vaudeville rule, "The show must go on." As William Lindsay Gresham writes:

> Houdini was used to minor injuries—cuts, bruises, abrasions, torn muscles, breaks, and strains—they were all alike to him. His way was to ignore them—get out there and give the folks a show.[69]

After the Albany performance, Houdini did get his ankle set, but he was up all night with the pain. He devised a special brace for his foot so that he could continue working, and he ordered his crew on to the next stop on the tour—Montreal, Canada.

## A Fatal Blow

In Montreal, another doctor advised Houdini to keep off the injured foot as much as possible. But he was determined to fulfill his obligations, which included a lecture on spiritualism at McGill University on October 21, 1926.

An undergraduate art major who attended the lecture made a sketch of Houdini and showed it to him afterward. Houdini was pleased with the work and invited the young man to visit him backstage before the next day's matinee performance.

At about 11 o'clock on the morning of October 22, the artist, Samuel J. Smiley, and two friends and fellow students, Jack Price and J. Gordon Whitehead, met Houdini in the lobby of the theater. Houdini escorted his guests to his dressing room.

Houdini took off his hat and coat, loosened his tie and shirt collar, and leaned back on a couch to sort through his mail while he chatted with his student admirers. One of the guests, Gordon Whitehead, was a large young man, over six feet tall and strongly built. He was an amateur boxer at the university.

Whitehead asked the famous magician if it were true that Houdini's regimen of clean living and regular exercise would let him receive the strongest blow a man could give him, on any portion of his body above the belt except the face. Houdini, still engrossed in his mail and only half-listening, affirmed that the statement was true. Whitehead then asked if he could punch Houdini in the stomach, and Houdini agreed.

Severely weakened through injury and lack of sleep, Houdini began to rise from the couch, but before he could tighten his stomach muscles—which would have prevented serious injury, even in his present condition—Whitehead struck him three times, very hard, in the abdomen.

Houdini fell back on the couch and the color drained from his face. The visitors were horrified, but Houdini, seeing their faces, managed to compose himself and mutter, "Not that way—got to get set for it."[70] The three students quickly left.

## The Last Shows

Despite extremely sore stomach muscles after the dressing-room incident, Houdini performed that afternoon. By evening, the pain was much worse. Bess tried to get her husband to see a doctor, but to no avail. The next day, October 23, he was fatigued and began experiencing chills and sweats, but he somehow forced his way through two performances.

That night, on the train en route to a two-week engagement in Detroit, Houdini's condition worsened. When the train stopped briefly in London, Ontario, Jim Collins wired Houdini's advance man in Detroit to have a doctor waiting at the station.

Houdini was immediately taken to his hotel room. He was running a fever of 102° F. The doctor told him that his appendix had ruptured. But Houdini had a sold-out crowd at the theater, and he refused to cancel.

The show that night, October 24, was to be his last. "There is such a thing as too much courage," biographer William Lindsay Gresham writes, "and Houdini showed it now. From the front, the audience could hardly suspect what was going on across the footlights. They were watching a dying man."[71] Somehow, miraculously, Houdini did make it through the entire show—and collapsed in the wings afterward.

He was taken to Detroit's Grace Hospital, where it was found that his appendix had developed gangrene. Advanced peritonitis, the severe inflammation of the abdominal area, had also set in. In the 1920s, before antibiotics, that diagnosis was virtually a death sentence.

## The End

Doctors operated on Houdini that night, and—although gravely ill—he clung to life for a few more days. Bess, still weak from her bout with food poisoning, took a turn for the worse and was given a room in the same hospital.

Apparently, Houdini was able to whisper a secret phrase to her, promising that he would try to speak it to her from beyond. The phrase was, "Rosabelle, believe." "Rosabelle" was the name of the

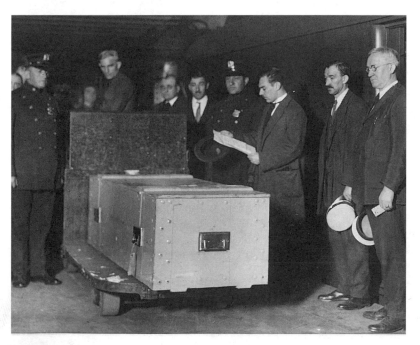

*Even the master of escapes was unable to escape the grip of death. A coffin that Houdini had prepared for an underwater escape holds his body after his death on October 31, 1926.*

song Bess had sung as part of her act on Coney Island, when she and Harry had met many years before.

Houdini's brothers Theo and Nat, and his sister Gladys, arrived from New York. Twice a day, the hospital issued bulletins about the famous patient. Houdini's illness made front-page news across the world. He underwent a second operation for further infection, but the doctors in charge of his case pronounced the results "less than favorable."

The end came quickly after that. Houdini's last words, spoken to Theo, were "I'm tired of fighting. . . . I guess this thing is going to get me."[72] Theo was still at the bedside when Houdini died, at 1:26 P.M. on October 31, 1926.

Contrary to popular belief, the bronze coffin in which Houdini's body was returned to New York City was not the one that had made headlines when the performer stayed underwater for an hour and a half in response to the challenge from Rahman Bey. It was, however, the elaborate coffin he had prepared for a touring version of that escape. A special Pullman car was engaged to carry the coffin home.

## The Funeral

A decade earlier, Houdini had left a sealed letter in a safe at the Elks Club in New York. It contained specific instructions for his funeral services and burial. The services were held in the Elks Lodge ballroom, on West 43rd Street, off Broadway.

Two thousand people attended the two-hour ceremony. One of the speakers, Rabbi Bernard Drachman, said, "He possessed a wondrous power which he never

understood and which he never revealed to anyone in life. He was one of the truly great men of our age." Added Rabbi B.A. Tintner, "He was exceptional, a unique personality, and besides that, he was one of the noblest and sweetest of men."[73]

A cedar wand was broken by a past president of the Society of American Magicians, and the members chanted these words:

> The curtain has at last been rung down. The wand is broken. God touched him with a wondrous gift and our brother made use of it. Now the wand is broken.[74]

Until Houdini's death, SAM had had no formal funeral rites; but with the passing of their most famous member, they began a new tradition. These rituals have been

*Thousands of fans pay their respects as Houdini's flower-laden casket passes by.*

*Bess visits her famous husband's grave one year after his death.*

used, in slightly modified form, at the funeral services of all SAM members ever since.

There were twenty-five cars in the funeral procession. Hundreds of thousands of mourners jammed the streets of New York, hoping for one last glimpse of the famous man.

Houdini was buried in Machpelah Cemetery on Long Island, next to his parents and one grandmother. His head rested on a pillow that contained his mother's letters. The tombstone is inscribed, "M.I. [most illustrious] President 1917-26," in honor of his service with the Society of American Magicians. SAM continues to maintain his gravestone.

There is one very curious aspect to Houdini's burial plot. Even after his death, Houdini managed to pull off one final, defiant stunt. A huge bust of the escape artist, designed by himself, was prominently displayed above his grave—in direct violation of Jewish custom, which does not permit images of the dead in cemeteries. Psychoanalyst and biographer Bernard C. Meyer commented that

> as an expression of . . . *chutzpah* [nerve], and as an exercise in magical ingenuity, Houdini's success in negotiating the admission of his chiseled likeness into a Jewish graveyard after his death ranks with the most spectacular escapes he effected during his lifetime.[75]

Sad to say, in 1975 vandals destroyed this bust.

In time, the entire family would be buried in this plot, with one exception. Even Houdini's brother Leopold, who had feuded bitterly with Houdini because he (Leopold) had scandalously married the former wife of another brother, was allowed into the burial plot.

The exception was Bess. She had wished to be buried alongside her husband; but when she died in 1943, her sister claimed that she had reembraced Catholicism at the last moment. Houdini's lifelong companion was instead buried in a nearby Catholic cemetery.

# The Mystery Lingers

Many rumors that circulated just after Houdini's death implied foul play. Was the man who had struck the fatal blows really a student? Was he truly unaware beforehand of just how much damage he could do? Was there a sinister motive behind the attack?

The New York Life Insurance Company, which had insured Houdini's life, cleared his death of any suspicion of foul play. The firm's investigators obtained signed statements from everyone who had been in the dressing room that day, as well as all the doctors who had treated Houdini. Nothing was found to indicate murder.

Houdini's lawyer estimated that Bess, the executor of Houdini's estate, would receive a small fortune in insurance. He also estimated that Bess would be a wealthy woman when Houdini's other assets were added up.

In fact, it was not so. Houdini left a number of outstanding debts when he died, and Bess was forced to sell the house on West 113th Street, along with her husband's collection of Lincoln holograph (original, signed) letters, thought to be the largest in the world.

Other parts of Houdini's estate went elsewhere; his library—some 5,200 volumes—was donated to the Library of Congress, and Theo received much of his extensive collection of magic equipment and memorabilia. By the time the debts were paid off, Bess was left with enough money to live comfortably, but she was by no means wealthy.

*Bess unveils a shrine to Houdini before attempting to contact her dead husband through a séance.*

## Secrets in the House

In Houdini's safe, Bess found the negatives of the photos in his scrapbooks and a note:

> Darling Wife and Loved One. In case you feel so disposed, destroy all of these negatives. I am not important or interesting enough for the world in general and so it's just as well you destroy them—unless you yourself either have a book written or write it yourself . . . otherwise destroy all film. Burn them. Your devoted husband, Houdini.[76]

The note was dated two months before he died.

Also in the safe was a thick pile of letters from women who'd fallen in love with Houdini over the years, out of personal friendship or from watching him perform. Although there is no evidence that he was ever unfaithful to Bess, he had kept the letters, apparently because they appealed to his vanity. Some time later, Bess gave a tea party for all the women who had written to Houdini. As each guest left she received a present—her letters, neatly tied up in ribbons.

## Life After Houdini

Even after she had finished grieving for her husband, Bess was lost. After all, she had spent thirty years of her life taking care of his every need. She briefly tried running a tea room in New York City, but her heart wasn't in it and the business didn't prosper. She thought about return-ing to show business with an act of her own, but never got serious about it. Never a heavy drinker, Bess now began to drink more than she ever had.

She was the widow of a world-famous man, however, and the public eye was constantly on her. Saddened and confused by Houdini's death, Bess became involved with a sordid scheme to exploit her fame.

A reporter for a tabloid-style newspaper, the New York *Graphic*, convinced Bess to put her name to a series of articles called "The Life and Loves of Houdini." The articles were to be written by the reporter but signed by Bess. But Bess angrily called the whole thing off when she

*After Houdini's death, Theo (professionally known as Hardeen) used his famous brother's name to promote his performances.*

## "A Magician Is Not a Juggler"

*In* Houdini: A
Mind in Chains,
*Bernard C. Meyer
comments on
Houdini's legacy.*

" 'A magician is not a juggler,' wrote the celebrated French conjurer, Robert-Houdin. 'He is an actor, playing a role—the role of a sorcerer.' Had Robert-Houdin been as richly favored with the gift of prophecy as he was in the art of conjuring, it might be supposed that [he] was foretelling the advent of his namesake Houdini, for in the annals of the art of necromancy [magic], no actor has been more acclaimed. Nor was Houdini a brief meteor that streaked across the sky only to turn to dust when new magicians caught the public eye. He belongs in the select company of those personages whose names are legendary throughout the world of entertainment: [the violinist Niccolò] Paganini, who was said to be in league with the Devil; [the actress] the Divine Sarah Bernhardt; Charlie Chaplin; and Babe Ruth, the Sultan of Swat. Others have equaled, and perhaps surpassed, the radiance of these stars, but few have eclipsed their fame or burned so bright an image on the public memory.

So it was with Houdini, the universal emblem of wizardry and illusion, whose immortality rests not on feats of sleight-of-hand, but on the magic of his presence and the spell of his charisma. As a conjurer, Houdini was undoubtedly outclassed by such virtuosi as Thurston, Blackstone, Dunninger, and other magicians. Indeed, he looked with evident disdain upon that designation, for he once told some newsmen, 'Don't insult me by calling me a magician. I am an escape artist.' "

became ill and the reporter brazenly tried to smuggle a photographer into her hospital room.

Meanwhile, a young spiritualist, the Reverend Arthur Ford, said he had contacted Houdini from beyond. He arranged a séance during which he claimed to have heard the secret password Houdini had given Bess when he died. The New York *Graphic*, angered by Bess's change of heart, tried to make it seem that Bess was planning a fraud in cahoots with Ford.

Late in her life, Bess moved to Los Angeles, where she met a man who would be her constant companion until her death.

*Bess makes a final attempt to communicate with the spirit of Houdini. Edward Saint holds Houdini's handcuffs.*

He was Edward Saint, a magician, mentalist, and psychic researcher. For many years, the couple held a quiet séance on the anniversary of Houdini's death, hoping to receive some word from him, and Bess never stopped believing that he might someday contact her.

But it was not to be. As she told the Los Angeles *Examiner* in 1935:

> I receive many messages that are supposed to come from Houdini through mediums and strange séances but they never mean anything to me. Very often I go to séances, hoping and praying that the signals Houdini gave me will be heard. No message comes to me while I am waiting to hear.[77]

Bess died of a heart attack on February 11, 1943, while on a train from California to New York. She apparently had no desire to come back from beyond the grave, having told friends, "When I go, I'll be gone for good. I won't even try to come back."[78] Houdini's brother Theo, who had returned to vaudeville, died in 1945.

## Lasting Legends

A number of truly fantastic legends have sprung up about Houdini in the years since his death. They give him supernatural powers and superhuman strength, and they help to keep his name alive. This would no doubt please Houdini greatly, since he was never shy of publicity that stretched the truth to the breaking point. As he once put it, "When I pass on, I would rather have one line in the press than a one-hundred-dollar wreath."[79]

One of the most enduring myths about Houdini stems from a jump he made into the Detroit River in the dead of winter.

The story goes that the river was frozen over, and Houdini arranged to have a hole cut in the ice. He jumped through it, cuffed hand and foot. After three minutes, however, the crowd anxiously lining the riverbanks saw no Houdini.

After five minutes, the reporters hurried back to report that Houdini was dead.

*The mystique that surrounds Houdini's life and death help keep his name alive.*

Surely no one could survive a freezing river that long! One of Houdini's aides threw down a rope and prepared to go down after him. But eight minutes after he'd plunged in, an arm broke through the frozen surface of the river—and then out came Houdini himself.

After being helped out and wrapped with blankets, Houdini explained what had happened. The river's current had swept him away from the hole. By the time he got his cuffs off, he could not find the opening. He survived only because he could swim to pockets of air that were trapped between the river and the ice. Breathing shallowly, he swam in a widening circle until he found the hole.

This tale was further enlivened by Bess's account in the "official" Kellock biography. She says she was so agitated by the thought of Houdini diving into the frozen river that she had returned to her hotel, rather than watch his certain death. Back in her room, she opened her window and overheard newsboys announcing Houdini's death! It was not until Houdini appeared on her doorstep, blue with cold and soaking wet, that she realized he was still alive.

It's a great story, but it's not true. According to the Detroit *News* of December 27, 1906, Houdini did jump from the bridge with two sets of handcuffs. But he was tied to a 113-foot lifeline, and the river was not frozen over. He jumped, got free of his shackles, and swam to a waiting lifeboat—an impressive feat, but not a superhuman one.

This is a perfect example of how Houdini's exploits have become amplified over time. When it came to his feats, Houdini himself was the biggest exaggerator of all. As magician-biographer Milbourne

*Houdini kept audiences spellbound with an ever changing array of stunts and escapes.*

Christopher has written, "Houdini himself is responsible for the most frequently retold fable about this feat."[80]

## The Legacy

Even disregarding the plainly fanciful tales, Houdini is still, without a doubt, the best-known name in magic. As the introductory quotation from Doug Henning suggests, if you stop a person at random on the street today—decades after Houdini's death—and ask for the first magician to come to mind, the answer will undoubtedly be Harry Houdini.

One reason is that Houdini's name has been kept alive by his admirers in the current generation. He has been a major inspiration to such noted modern illusionists as Henning, David Copperfield, and the Amazing Randi. By reproducing or adapting the performances that made Houdini famous, they keep the art of magic before the public and, at the same time, honor their famous predecessor.

It is not because of Houdini's sheer skill that he remains famous. He was not the most skillful magician who ever lived. Historians of magic generally agree that for pure dexterity, the world has seen more impressive illusionists both before and after him. As William Lindsay Gresham notes, "At straight magic he was often strangely inept. At his specialty he was magnificent."[81]

Houdini's lasting fame results in part from his genius for publicity. He was brilliant at staging innovative stunts that attracted reporters and audiences, and he was tireless in his efforts to keep the name

## Stormy Living

*In* Houdini: The Man Who Walked Through Walls, *William Lindsay Gresham reflects on the odd mixture of human and superhuman in Houdini's legacy.*

"All that remains of Houdini now are the files of letters, the trunks of handcuffs and keys, the stored apparatus with which he 'cast the glamourie.' But the legend promises to live when all the handcuffs have been devoured by rust.

Into fifty-two years, he packed enough stormy living for a dozen lifetimes. . . . At straight magic he was often strangely inept. At his specialty he was magnificent. He was an expert underwater swimmer and high diver, a master lock-picker, a pioneer aviator, magical historian, movie stunt man, psychic investigator, author and editor, genius of publicity, intimate of presidents, entertainer of kings, vaudeville headline for twenty years. He was charitable and vindictive, generous and penny-pinching; like a little boy he would forget to wash his ears and change his clothes. . . . He never refused to play a benefit, without pay, for the inmates of asylums and prisons. Too vain to wear glasses in his later years, he carried a magnifying glass for casual reading. A nonsmoker, he kept his fingers busy by rolling a half dollar over and over his knuckles, one of the most difficult flourishes in magic. He was too absent-minded to drive a car. Fascinated by cemeteries, he extended his grave-visiting to the tombs of his friends' parents. Athlete and showman, collector and pamphleteer, Houdini lives on in legend noted for but one thing: To the generations that have risen since his death he is 'the man who walked through walls.'"

of Houdini before the public. He also reached the peak of his popularity just as radio was about to change the world, and he pioneered the use of the new technology for publicity purposes.

The legend has also been fueled by persistent rumors that Houdini took a mysterious, all-powerful secret to the grave. Reports of buried codes and hidden clues in the stones and inscriptions of his grave continue to appear from time to time. As recently as 1975 his name was in headlines around the world, when his stone bust in the family burial plot was smashed to pieces. Bernard C. Meyer, in *Houdini: A Mind in Chains*, writes:

Although neither the perpetrator of this act of vandalism nor its motive was identified, it offers renewed affirmation of the enduring vitality of [Houdini's] spirit and of his unfailing ability to rouse the public passions.[82]

Only so many concrete reasons, however, can be given to explain Houdini's continuing popularity. There is also something enduringly mysterious about his legacy. No one knows exactly why Houdini is still as famous today as he was in his prime. In an age of high-tech wonders and information overload, it is indeed something of a mystery that Houdini's name survives. And yet it does.

Houdini's legend today is an odd mixture of the very human and the almost superhuman. His voluminous scrapbooks are on file at the Library of Congress, and his enormous collections of handcuffs, keys, magic apparatus, and other memorabilia are scattered about—some in private collections and some at the Houdini Magical Hall of Fame in Niagara Falls, Ontario. In addition, many books are available that discuss his life and work in detail.

But these are tangible items. The intangible part of Houdini's legend—the memory of his mystery, secrecy, courage, and bravado—will remain long after these mementos have turned to dust, because he lives on in our collective imagination. As Milbourne Christopher has written:

Scarcely a day goes by without [his name] appearing somewhere in the press of the world. Anyone who does something remarkable is labeled a Houdini, whether he escapes from a famous prison or makes a fantastic catch during a baseball game. No other mystery worker has ever appealed so much to the public's imagination.[83]

# Notes

## Introduction: The Best-Remembered Magician

1. Doug Henning with Charles Reynolds, *Houdini: His Legend and His Magic.* New York: New York Times Books, 1977.
2. Milbourne Christopher, *Houdini, the Untold Story.* New York: Crowell, 1969.
3. Quoted in William Lindsay Gresham, *Houdini: The Man Who Walked Through Walls.* New York: Holt, 1959.
4. Quoted in Christopher, *Houdini, the Untold Story.*
5. Quoted in Christopher, *Houdini, the Untold Story.*

## Chapter 1: Houdini's Early Life

6. Harold Kellock, *Houdini: His Life Story.* New York: Harcourt, Brace, 1928.
7. Bernard C. Meyer, *Houdini: A Mind in Chains: A Psychoanalytic Portrait.* New York: Dutton, 1976.
8. Quoted in Henning with Reynolds, *Houdini: His Legend and His Magic.*
9. Quoted in Christopher, *Houdini, the Untold Story.*
10. Quoted in Christopher, *Houdini, the Untold Story.*

## Chapter 2: The Beginnings of a Career

11. Christopher, *Houdini, the Untold Story.*
12. Quoted in Christopher, *Houdini, the Untold Story.*
13. Quoted in Christopher, *Houdini, the Untold Story.*
14. Quoted in Gresham, *Houdini: The Man Who Walked Through Walls.*
15. Quoted in Christopher, *Houdini, the Untold Story.*
16. Quoted in Gresham, *Houdini: The Man Who Walked Through Walls.*
17. Quoted in Christopher, *Houdini, the Untold Story.*
18. Quoted in Gresham, *Houdini: The Man Who Walked Through Walls.*

## Chapter 3: Europe and Return

19. Quoted in Christopher, *Houdini, the Untold Story.*
20. Quoted in Christopher, *Houdini, the Untold Story.*
21. Gresham, *Houdini: The Man Who Walked Through Walls.*
22. Quoted in Christopher, *Houdini, The Untold Story.*

23. Quoted in Christopher, *Houdini, the Untold Story.*
24. Christopher, *Houdini, the Untold Story.*
25. Quoted in Christopher, *Houdini, the Untold Story.*
26. Gresham, *Houdini: The Man Who Walked Through Walls.*
27. Quoted in Gresham, *Houdini: The Man Who Walked Through Walls.*
28. Quoted in Christopher, *Houdini, the Untold Story.*
29. Quoted in Meyer, *Houdini: A Mind in Chains.*

## Chapter 4: From Magician to Escape Artist

30. Quoted in Gresham, *Houdini: The Man Who Walked Through Walls.*
31. Quoted in Christopher, *Houdini, the Untold Story.*
32. Quoted in Christopher, *Houdini, the Untold Story.*
33. Quoted in Gresham, *Houdini: The Man Who Walked Through Walls.*
34. Houdini, quoted in *Houdini on Magic*, edited by Walter B. Gibson and Morris N. Young. New York: Dover, 1953.
35. Gresham, *Houdini: The Man Who Walked Through Walls.*
36. Quoted in Kellock, *Houdini: His Life Story.*
37. Quoted in Walter B. Gibson, editor, *Houdini's Escapes and Magic.* New York: Funk and Wagnalls, 1976.
38. Quoted in Gibson and Young, editors, *Houdini on Magic.*
39. Quoted in Gresham, *Houdini: The Man Who Walked Through Walls.*
40. Quoted in Christopher, *Houdini, the Untold Story.*
41. Quoted in Christopher, *Houdini, the Untold Story.*
42. Gresham, *Houdini: The Man Who Walked Through Walls.*
43. Quoted in Christopher, *Houdini, the Untold Story.*
44. Quoted in Christopher, *Houdini, the Untold Story.*
45. Christopher, *Houdini, the Untold Story.*
46. Quoted in Christopher, *Houdini, the Untold Story.*

## Chapter 5: Magic and Movies: During and After the War

47. Quoted in Christopher, *Houdini, the Untold Story.*

48. Gibson, editor, *Houdini's Escapes and Magic.*

49. Quoted in Christopher, *Houdini, the Untold Story.*

50. Quoted in Christopher, *Houdini, the Untold Story.*

51. Quoted in Henning with Reynolds, *Houdini: His Legend and His Magic.*

52. Quoted in Henning with Reynolds, *Houdini: His Legend and His Magic.*

53. Christopher, *Houdini, the Untold Story.*

## Chapter 6: Exposing Spiritualism

54. Gresham, *Houdini: The Man Who Walked Through Walls.*

55. Quoted in Gibson and Young, editors, *Houdini on Magic.*

56. Quoted in Christopher, *Houdini, the Untold Story.*

57. Christopher, *Houdini, the Untold Story.*

58. Christopher, *Houdini, the Untold Story.*

59. Quoted in Christopher, *Houdini, the Untold Story.*

60. Quoted in Christopher, *Houdini, the Untold Story.*

61. Quoted in Gresham, *Houdini: The Man Who Walked Through Walls.*

62. Quoted in Gresham, *Houdini: The Man Who Walked Through Walls.*

63. Quoted in Christopher, *Houdini, the Untold Story.*

64. Quoted in Christopher, *Houdini, the Untold Story.*

65. Quoted in Christopher, *Houdini, the Untold Story.*

66. Quoted in Christopher, *Houdini, the Untold Story.*

## Chapter 7: Houdini's Last Days

67. Quoted in Meyer, *Houdini: A Mind in Chains.*

68. Quoted in Christopher, *Houdini, the Untold Story.*

69. Gresham, *Houdini: The Man Who Walked Through Walls.*

70. Quoted in Gresham, *Houdini: The Man Who Walked Through Walls.*

71. Gresham, *Houdini: The Man Who Walked Through Walls.*

72. Quoted in Gresham, *Houdini: The Man Who Walked Through Walls.*

73. Quoted in Christopher, *Houdini, the Untold Story.*

74. Quoted in Christopher, *Houdini, the Untold Story.*

75. Meyer, *Houdini: A Mind in Chains.*

## Epilogue: The Mystery Lingers

76. Quoted in Christopher, *Houdini, the Untold Story.*

77. Quoted in Gresham, *Houdini: The Man Who Walked Through Walls.*

78. Quoted in Christopher, *Houdini, the Untold Story.*

79. Quoted in Henning with Reynolds, *Houdini: His Legend and His Magic.*

80. Christopher, *Houdini, the Untold Story.*

81. Gresham, *Houdini: The Man Who Walked Through Walls.*

82. Meyer, *Houdini: A Mind in Chains.*

83. Christopher, *Houdini, the Untold Story.*

# For Further Reading

Milbourne Christopher, *Houdini, the Untold Story*. New York: Thomas Crowell, 1969. The most complete and authoritative biography, by a magician who knew Houdini and is the recognized authority on him.

Walter B. Gibson, editor, *Houdini's Escapes and Magic*. New York: Funk and Wagnalls, 1976. A collection of explanations, mostly by Houdini himself, that detail many of his escapes and magic tricks.

William Lindsay Gresham, *Houdini: The Man Who Walked Through Walls*. New York: Henry Holt, 1959. Less thorough than Christopher and with occasional errors, but also well written, with many excellent anecdotes about its subject.

Doug Henning with Charles Reynolds, *Houdini: His Legend and His Magic*. New York: New York Times Books, 1977. Long, dry sections on the myth of the magician-hero through time, and with little biographical information to add—but the single best source of visual material on Houdini. Many pages of fascinating photos, scrapbook entries, old handbills, and other memorabilia.

Harry Houdini, edited by Walter B. Gibson and Morris N. Young, *Houdini On Magic*. New York: Dover, 1953. Reprints of pieces written by Houdini on the history of magic and other subjects, with introductory notes by the editors.

Harold Kellock, *Houdini: His Life Story*. New York: Harcourt, Brace, 1928. The "official" story, written with the collaboration of Bess Houdini shortly after her husband's death; highly embellished and written in a flowery style.

Beryl Williams and Samuel Epstein, *The Great Houdini, Magician Extraordinary*. New York: Julian Messner, 1950. Simply written for young adults, but full of errors and whitewashing.

# Additional Works Consulted

J.C. Cannell, *The Secrets of Houdini*. Ann Arbor, MI.: Gryphon Books, 1971. Written by a British magician and historian who purports to explain some of Houdini's best-known tricks.

Raymund FitzSimons, *Death and the Magician*. New York: Atheneum, 1980. The most recently published biography, but adds little to the Christopher and Gresham books.

Bernard C. Meyer, MD, *Houdini: A Mind in Chains: A Psychoanalytic Portrait*. New York: Dutton, 1976. Dry and pompous, written by a Freudian analyst with no apparent sense of humor, but with fascinating insights nonetheless into the darker side of its subject.

# Index

Aerial League of Australia, 57

Alhambra Theater (London), 32, 34

Amazing Randi, the, 9, 85, 99

American Society for Psychical Research, 80

Anderson, John Henry, 59

Baldwin, Samri (the White Mahatma), 23, 32

*Baltimore Sun*, 89

Barnum, P. T., 19

Bean Giant handcuffs, 32

Beck, Martin, 27

Becks, Alfred, 65

benefits and free shows, 64-65

Bey, Rahman, 84-85

Bird, J. Malcolm, 81

Bosco (magician), 53

brick wall trick, 57-58

British College of Psychic Science, 79

Brothers Houdini, the, 18, 19-21

buried alive stunt, 85

California Concert Company, 26

challenges of and to Houdini, 28, 32, 33, 57, 68

channelers, 73

Chatham Naval Barracks challenge, 57

Chicago World's Fair, 18

Chinese torture cell escape, 45, 86-87

Christopher, Milbourne, 42, 46, 62, 71, 89

on Houdini and spiritualism, 75, 76

on Houdini's lasting impact, 101

on reason for Houdini's appeal, 10

on vaudeville, 19, 20

on Weiss family reunion, 36

on young Houdini's job-application technique, 15

*Cincinnati Commercial Tribune*, 76

Cirnoc, P. H., 32, 34

collections and library of Houdini, 59, 65-66, 94

Collins, Jim, 55, 58, 91

Colosseum Theater (Essen, Germany), 35

Columbian Exposition, 18

Coney Island, 18, 21

*Conjuror's Monthly*, 49

Copperfield, David (magician), 9, 99

Crandon, Le Roi Goddard, 80-81

Crandon, Mina, 81

Dale, Alan, 46

darbies (handcuffs), 34

Day, Harry, 32

De Kolta, Buatier, 61

*Detroit News*, 98

disappearing elephant trick, 45, 61-62

Downs, T. Nelson (King of Koins), 31-32

Doyle, Lady (Mrs. Arthur Conan), 78-79

Doyle, Sir Arthur Conan, 77-80

Drachman, Bernard, 92

*Essener Volkszeitung*, 35

"Expanding Cube" illusion, 61

Floral Sisters, the, 21

Ford, Rev. Arthur, 96

Gans, Arthur, 54

Garfield, James A., 47

giant football escape, 51

Gibson, Walter B., 28, 41, 73, 79

on Houdini and history of magic, 51

on Houdini's notes and writings, 64, 68

on Houdini's showmanship, 50

Goldston, Will, 41

Goshen, Colonel, 20

Graff (German policeman), 38

Great Alexander (magician), 57

Gresham, William Lindsay, 53, 55, 57, 99

on failure of Houdini's movies, 71

on Houdini's appeal in Germany, 35

on Houdini's legacy, 100

on Houdini's pain and courage, 90, 91

on Houdini's

showmanship, 29
*The Grim Game* (movie), 67-69
Guiteau, Charles J., 47

*Haldane of the Secret Service* (movie), 69-70
Hammerstein's Roof Garden (theater), 49
handcuff escapes, 23, 39, 42
*Handcuff Secrets* (Houdini), 53
Hardeen. *See* Weisz (Weiss), Theodore
Hayman, Jacob (Jack), 16, 18
Henning, Doug, 9, 11, 99
Herrman the Great (magician), 44
Hippodrome (London), 42
history of magic
Houdini and, 51
Houdini, Bess (wife of Houdini), 26, 71, 90, 93
as Beatrice Raymond, 20-21
born Wilhelmina Rahner, 20
death, 97
her life after Houdini, 94-97
illness of, 87-88
marriage, 22
on Houdini's superstitions, 74
returns to stage with Houdini, 60-61
with Houdini as The Rahners—Sparkling Comedy Team, 30
Houdini, Harry
Arthur Conan Doyle and, 78-80
as collector, 59, 65-66, 94

as King of Handcuffs, 24, 30
as pilot, 56-57
as "the Prince of the Air," 12
athletic ability of, 15-16
Australian tour, 55-57
beer can stunt almost fatal, 57
benefits and free shows given by, 64-65
born Ehrich Weiss (Weisz), 12-16
challenges, 28, 32, 33, 57, 68
changes his name, 16, 18
court trials in Europe, 38
death and funeral, 92-93
early years, 12-16
early jobs, 14, 15
first performance, 14
ran away for a year, 14-15
ego problems of, 53-55
European success, 31-44
exposure of spiritualism, 72-85
government testimony, 82
opinions on spiritualism, 75, 77, 79, 83
*Scientific American* committee, 80-81
$10,000 reward and, 73
fatal blow and last shows, 90-91
handcuff duel with Kleppini, 38-40
history of magic and, 51
in Germany, 34-36
jealousy of other magicians, 49
lasting appeal, reasons

for, 10-11
London failure and success, 32-34
marriage, 22
memorization ability of, 26-27
mother's death, impact of, 58-59
movie career of, 66-71
on secret of success, 64
on straitjacket escape method, 54
personality characteristics, 10
physical description, 10
psyching out audiences, 40-42
publicity, knack for, 11, 23-24, 99-100
"Naked Test," 29-30
published works
*Handcuff Secrets*, 53
*A Magician Among the Spirits*, 75
*The Right Way to Do Wrong*, 48
*The Unmasking of Robert-Houdin*, 39
Russian successes, 42-43
seasickness problems, 25-26, 32, 55
showmanship
as master of, 50
opinions on, 41
superstitions of, 74
Theo as partner, 18-21
timeline of life, 8
tricks/acts/escapes
bank vault escapes, 41
brick wall trick, 57-58
Chinese torture cell escape, 45, 86-87
disappearing elephant trick, 45, 61-62

escapes from various trusses, 51

"Expanding Cube" illusion, 61

giant football escape, 51

handcuff escapes, 23, 39, 42

jail cell escapes, 34, 47-48

"Metamorphosis" trick, 20, 27

milk (water) can escapes, 51, 57

sealed coffin escape, 84-85

"second-sight" mind reading, 23, 64

spirit show, 26

straitjacket escapes, 24-25, 29, 45, 50

method of, 54

upside down and trussed, 61-63

threaded-needle trick, 88

underwater packing crate escape, 48-49

wet packs escape, 52

with Bess as The Rahners—Sparkling Comedy Team, 30

Houdini Brothers, the (act), 18, 19-21

*Houdini: A Mind in Chains: A Psychoanalytic Portrait* (Meyer), 12, 17, 39, 96, 100-101

*Houdini: His Legend and His Magic* (Henning), 11

*Houdini: His Life Story* (Kellock), 12, 22, 53, 64, 74

Houdini Magical Hall of Fame, 101

*Houdini on Magic* (Gibson and Young, eds.), 41, 68

*Houdini: The Man Who Walked Through Walls* (Gresham), 100

*Houdini: The Untold Story* (Christopher), 15, 19, 33, 46, 62, 83, 89

*Houdini's Escapes and Magic* (Gibson, ed.), 28, 50, 53, 54, 79

H. Richters' Sons, 15

Huber's Museum, 18

Imperial Music Hall (New York), 20

jail cell escapes, 34, 47-48

methods used, 47

Jarrow, Emil, 18

Kammsetzer (theater manager), 34-35

Keith circuit, 29

Kellar, Harry, 9, 16, 18, 53

Kellock, Harold, 12, 22, 64, 74, 98

King of Koins (T. Nelson Downs), 31-32

Kleppini (magician) handcuff duel, 38-40

Kukol, Franz, 37, 57, 60

Library of Congress, 94, 101

Lincoln, Abraham, letters of, 94

*London Daily Mirror,* 42

*London Telegraph,* 84

*Los Angeles Examiner,* 97

Lovecraft, H. P., 69

Lynn, Dr. (magician), 14

Lyric Theater (Asbury Park), 58

Machpelah Cemetery, 44, 58, 93

Mackenzie, J. Hewat, 79

*A Magician Among the Spirits* (Houdini), 75

Magicians' Club (London), 54, 55, 59

*The Man from Beyond* (movie), 69-70

"Margery" case, 80-81

*The Master Mystery* (movie serial), 66-67

Mellini (magician), 44

*The Memoirs of Robert-Houdin, Ambassador, Author, Conjuror, Written by Himself,* 16

"Metamorphosis" trick, 20, 27

Meyer, Bernard C., 12, 17, 39, 93, 96, 100-101

milk (water) can escapes, 51, 57

*Milwaukee Journal,* 14

movie career of Houdini, 66-71

"Naked Test," 29-30

Naldi, Mito, 71

*New York American,* 46

*New York Clipper,* 65

*New York Graphic,* 95-96

New York Life Insurance Company, 94

*New York Morning Telegraph,* 82

*New York World,* 76

Nicholas, czar of Russia, 42

Orpheum circuit, 27-29

Pantages circuit, 29

Pastime Athletic Club, 16

Price, Jack, 90

"the Prince of the Air" (Houdini), 12
Providence Opera House, 88

Rahner, Mrs. (Bess's mother), 49
Rahner, Wilhelmina. *See* Houdini, Bess
The Rahners—Sparkling Comedy Team, 30
Raymond, Beatrice. *See* Houdini, Bess
Rickards, Harry, 55
*The Right Way to Do Wrong* (Houdini), 48
Robert-Houdin, Jean Eugène, 9, 16, 37-39, 44, 96
Roosevelt, Theodore, 82-84

Saint, Edward, 97
SAM. *See* Society of American Magicians
*San Francisco Examiner*, 27-29
Sawyer, Julia, 76-77
*Scientific American*
committee on spiritualism, 80-81
Scotland Yard escape, 34
sealed coffin escape, 84-85
"second-sight" mind reading act, 23, 64
Siberia wagon escape, 43
Smiley, Samuel J., 90
Society of American Magicians (SAM), 43, 44, 53, 93-94
*Spirit Intercourse* (Mackenzie), 79
spirit mediums, 73
spirit photographs, 80

spirit show, 26
spiritualism
exposure of, 72-85
Houdini on, 75, 77, 79, 83
Steiner, Cecilia. *See* Weisz (Weiss), Cecilia Steiner
straitjacket escapes, 24-25, 29, 45, 50
Houdini on method, 54
upside down and trussed, 61-63
substitution trick, 20, 61
superstitions of Houdini, 74

*Terror Island* (movie), 69
threaded-needle trick, 88
Tintner, B. A., 92

underwater packing crate escape, 48-49
*The Unmasking of Robert-Houdin* (Houdini), 39
Unthan, The Legless Wonder, 20

vanishing elephant trick, 45, 61-62
*Variety*, 62
Vickery, Jim, 55
Victoria, queen of England, 36
"The Village Blacksmith" (Longfellow), 16

water (milk) can escapes, 51, 57
Weiss (Weisz), Ehrich. *See* Houdini, Harry
Weisz (Weiss), Armin (Herman; half brother of Houdini), 13, 44

Weisz (Weiss), Cecilia Steiner (mother of Houdini), 13-14, 22, 49
death, 58
watches son in Hamburg, 36
Weisz (Weiss), Gladys (sister of Houdini), 13, 58, 92
Weisz (Weiss), Leopold (brother of Houdini), 13, 39, 93
Weisz (Weiss), Mayer Samuel (father of Houdini), 13-15, 18, 44
Weisz (Weiss), Nathan (brother of Houdini), 13, 92
Weisz (Weiss), Theodore (Theo; brother of Houdini), 13, 15, 58, 69, 87
as Hardeen, 22
death, 97
early partner of Houdini, 18-21
received Houdini's collection, 94, 95
Weisz (Weiss), William (brother of Houdini), 13
Welsh Brothers Circus, 23, 27
wet packs escape, 52
Whitehead, J. Gordon, 90
Willat, Irvin, 68
Wilson, Edmund, 11
Wilson, Woodrow, 11

Zancigs, the (psychic couple), 80

# Picture Credits

Cover photo by UPI/Bettmann

AP/Wide World, 94, 97

The Bettmann Archive, 16, 18, 25 (left), 35, 51, 63 (both), 66 (top), 69 (left), 75, 83

Marie Blood, 21 (top)

Brown Brothers, 40, 50, 52, 86

Frank W. Dailey, 9, 10, 13 (left), 21 (bottom), 47, 66 (bottom)

Library of Congress, 13 (right), 19, 24, 25 (right), 26, 29, 31, 32, 36, 37, 43, 45, 48, 49 (all), 56, 59, 61, 67, 69 (right), 70 (both), 71, 73, 82, 85 (both), 87, 88, 95

Stock Montage, Inc., 27, 30

UPI/Bettmann, 60, 72, 78, 81, 91, 92, 93, 98, 99

# About the Author

Adam Woog, a lifelong fan of magicians and vaudeville performers, lives in Seattle, Washington, with his wife and daughter. He writes often about the Pacific Northwest and is the author of two books of regional history: *Sexless Oysters and Self-Tipping Hats: 100 Years of Invention in the Pacific Northwest* and *Atomic Marbles and Branding Irons: Museums, Collections, and Roadside Curiosities of Washington and Oregon.*